Mary Helen Allies, Saint John of Damascus

St. John Damascene on Holy Images

Three Sermons on the Assumption

Mary Helen Allies, Saint John of Damascus

St. John Damascene on Holy Images
Three Sermons on the Assumption

ISBN/EAN: 9783744691567

Printed in Europe, USA, Canada, Australia, Japan

Cover: Foto ©ninafisch / pixelio.de

More available books at **www.hansebooks.com**

ST JOHN DAMASCENE

Imprimatur

HERBERTUS CARDINALIS VAUGHAN
ARCHIEPISCOPUS WESTMONASTERIENSIS

Die 12 Augusti 1898

ST JOHN DAMASCENE

ON

HOLY IMAGES

(πρὸς τοὺς διαβάλλοντας τὰς ἁγίας εἰκόνας)

FOLLOWED BY

THREE SERMONS ON THE ASSUMPTION
(κοίμησις)

TRANSLATED FROM THE ORIGINAL GREEK

BY

MARY H. ALLIES

London
THOMAS BAKER
1 SOHO SQUARE, W.

1898

TRANSLATOR'S PREFACE

A Treatise on Images will not be out of place in a public, which is confusing the making of images with the making of idols. A great Christian of the eighth century found himself called upon to face an imperial Iconoclast. He would willingly have remained silent, but he would not bury his talent of eloquence. He brought it forth and witnessed to the teaching of the Church in language which present 'exciting scenes' in Anglican churches brings home in the most forcible way. Our English image breakers are in the camp of Leo the Isaurian, who in the eighth century waged war against holy images, on the plausible pretext that they withdrew honour from God. The seventh General Council condemned his assault, and it determined the different kinds of worship, using the Greek terms of latreia and douleia. The special champion of holy Images is St John Damascene, whose treatise is now published for the first time in English. Every article in the creed has its special defender. St John Damascene proclaims the Communion of Saints and the honour of God through His chosen and favoured servants. No part of Catholic belief is a vain word, nor can the true children of the Church say with their lips what they do not hold in their hearts. I believe in the Communion of Saints follows upon I believe in God, so that the enemies of the Saints are the enemies of God. This is the doctrine which St John Damascene traces back to the eternal ages before time was, in the divine εἰκων of the Father in the Person of the Son. God, the Son, is the Image by essence, and then He becomes a visible image or form in time, clothed in flesh and blood, showing us by His own example that our worship of God is through corporeal things. Again and again the Saint repeats that as we must not make an image of the Invisible God, so neither must we refuse to look upon the Son, His Image, first in eternity, and then Incarnate.

What are the consequences of rejecting divinely appointed images? Hopeless and heart-destroying doubt caused by the undue exaltation of humanity : in other words, creature, instead of divine, worship. We are so constituted that images we must have : our minds cannot reach God's throne without the help of corporeal things. Agnosticism has said it. We cannot love what we do not know, and is not God unknowable? Halting formularies say it when they point to matter, which God has glorified, as inglorious. And halting formularies lead to halting souls, and to the proclamation of the strange device that religious truth is of no consequence so long as men lead good lives.

The sermons on the Assumption were preached by the Saint in or about A.D. 727. According to Alban Butler, he had special reasons for honouring the Mother of God. By her intercession he regained the use of his strong right hand. It was a practical demonstration of Catholic teaching, We reach God most surely through those who love Him best, and thus the Protestant phrase, which expresses a purely Catholic thought 'straight to God,' is exemplified in the Communion of Saints. St John's language about the Θεοτοκη will astonish those who stigmatise the love of her as a 'Roman corruption.' The crowning triumph of the Assumption follows justly on the divine maternity. Her body was all pure, because her all holy (παναγία) soul made it the resting-place of our Lord. The Mother is so identified with the Son that her life is part of His. The tomb is not for her, and thus the writer of the eighth century bears full testimony to Catholic tradition.

All believers are at one in wishing to reach God; the question is one of detail. Which is the shortest road? St John Damascene speaks with the Church when he says it is through the glorification of matter in the Person of the Eternal Word. Either give matter its proper place, or take away matter which the Lord Himself has exalted, and we are no longer composite beings, but spirits ill at ease in a material world. Take away the King's army, and you uncrown the King Himself. Forget His Mother, and with her the connecting link between earth and heaven. Then we may be heathens once more, groping after the unknown God, and our latter state will be more appalling than the heathendom of old, before the light had appeared to illumine earth's dark places.

CONTENTS

		PAGE
PART I.	APOLOGIA OF ST JOHN DAMASCENE AGAINST THOSE WHO DECRY HOLY IMAGES	1
,, II.	THE SAME	55
,, III.	THE SAME	87
SERMON I.	ON THE ASSUMPTION	147
,, II.	THE SAME	171
,, III.	THE SAME	201

PART I.

APOLOGIA OF ST JOHN DAMASCENE AGAINST THOSE WHO DECRY HOLY IMAGES.

WITH the ever-present conviction of my own unworthiness, I ought to have kept silence and confessed my shortcomings before God, but all things are good at the right time. I see the Church which God founded on the Apostles and Prophets, its corner-stone being Christ His Son, tossed on an angry sea, beaten by rushing waves, shaken and troubled by the assaults of evil spirits. I see rents in the seamless robe of Christ, which impious men have sought to part asunder, and His body cut into pieces, that is, the word of God and the ancient tradition of the Church. Therefore I have judged it unreasonable to keep silence and to hold my tongue, bearing in mind the Scripture warning:—'If thou withdrawest thyself, my soul shall not delight in thee,' and 'If thou seest the sword coming and dost not warn thy brother, I shall require his blood at thy hand.' Fear, then, compelled me to speak; the truth was stronger than the majesty of kings. 'I bore testimony to Thee before kings,' I heard the royal* David saying, 'and I was' not ashamed. No, I was the more incited to speak. The King's command is all powerful over his subjects. For few men have hitherto been found who, whilst recognising the power of the earthly king to come from above, have resisted his unlawful demands.

In the first place, grasping as a kind of pillar, or foundation, the teaching of the Church, which is our salvation, I have opened out its meaning, giving, as it were, the reins to a well-caparisoned charger.† For I look upon it as a great calamity that the Church, adorned with her great privileges and the holiest examples of saints in the past, should go back to the first rudiments, and fear where there is no fear. It is disastrous to suppose that the Church does not know God as He is, that she degenerates into idolatry, for if she declines from perfection

---

* Θεοπατωρ, not easily rendered in English.

† Καὶ τοῦτον ὥσπερ ἵππον εὐχάλινον, τῆς ἀφετηρίας παρώρμησα.

in a single iota, it is as an enduring mark on a comely face, destroying by its unsightliness the beauty of the whole. A small thing is not small when it leads to something great, nor indeed is it a thing of no matter to give up the ancient tradition of the Church held by our forefathers, whose conduct we should observe, and whose faith we should imitate.

In the first place, then, before speaking to you, I beseech Almighty God, to whom all things lie open, who knows my small capacity and my genuine intention, to bless the words of my mouth, and to enable me to bridle my mind and direct it to Him, to walk in His presence straightly, not declining to a plausible right hand, nor knowing the left. Then I ask all God's people, the chosen ones of His royal priesthood, with the holy shepherd of Christ's orthodox flock, who represents in his own person Christ's priesthood, to receive my treatise with kindness. They must not dwell on my unworthiness, nor seek for eloquence, for I am only too conscious of my shortcomings. They must consider the thoughts themselves. The kingdom of heaven is not in word but in deed. Conquest is not my object. I raise a hand which is fighting for the truth—a willing hand under the divine guidance. Relying, then, upon substantial truth as my auxiliary, I will enter on my subject matter.

I have taken heed to the words of Truth Himself:—'The Lord thy God is one.' And 'Thou shalt fear the Lord thy God, and shalt serve Him only, and thou shalt not have strange gods.' Again, 'Thou shalt not make to thyself a graven thing, nor the likeness of anything that is in heaven above, or in the earth beneath'; and 'Let them be all confounded that adore graven things.' Again, 'The gods that have not made heaven and earth, let them perish.' In this way God spoke of old to the patriarchs through the prophets, and lastly, through His only-begotten Son, on whose account He made the ages. He says, 'This is eternal life, that they may know Thee, the only true God, and Jesus Christ whom Thou didst send.' I believe in one God, the source of all things, without beginning, uncreated, immortal, everlasting, incomprehensible, bodiless, invisible, uncircumscribed,* without form. I believe in one supersubstantial

* ἀπερίγραπτος, *i.e.*, not in place.

being, one divine Godhead in three entities, the Father, the Son, and the Holy Ghost, and I adore Him alone with the worship of latreia. I adore one God, one Godhead but three Persons, God the Father, God the Son made flesh, and God the Holy Ghost, one God. I do not adore creation more than the Creator, but I adore the creature created as I am, adopting creation freely and spontaneously that He might elevate our nature and make us partakers of His divine nature. Together with my Lord and King I worship Him clothed in the flesh, not as if it were a garment or He constituted a fourth person of the Trinity—God forbid. That flesh is divine, and endures after its assumption. Human nature was not lost in the Godhead, but just as the Word made flesh remained the Word, so flesh became the Word remaining flesh, becoming, rather, one with the Word through union (καθ' ὑπος-τασιν). Therefore I venture to draw an image of the invisible God, not as invisible, but as having become visible for our sakes through flesh and blood. I do not draw an image of the immortal Godhead. I paint the visible flesh of God, for it is impossible to represent a spirit (ψυχή), how much more God who gives breath to the spirit.

Now adversaries say: God's commands to Moses the law-giver were, 'Thou shalt adore the Lord thy God, and thou shalt worship him alone, and thou shalt not make to thyself a graven thing that is in heaven above, or in the earth beneath.'

They err truly, not knowing the Scriptures, for the letter kills whilst the spirit quickens—not finding in the letter the hidden meaning. I could say to these people, with justice, He who taught you this would teach you the following. Listen to the law-giver's interpretation in Deuteronomy: 'And the Lord spoke to you from the midst of the fire. You heard the voice of His words, but you saw not any form at all.' And shortly afterwards: 'Keep your souls carefully. You saw not any similitude in the day that the Lord God spoke to you in Horeb from the midst of the fire, lest perhaps being deceived you might make you a graven similitude, or image of male and female, the similitude of any beasts that are upon the earth, or of birds that fly under heaven.' And again, 'Lest, perhaps, lifting up thy eyes to heaven, thou see the sun and the moon, and all the stars of heaven, and being deceived by error thou adore and serve them.'

You see the one thing to be aimed at is not to adore a created thing more than the Creator, nor to give the worship of latreia except to Him alone. By worship, consequently, He always understands the worship of latreia. For, again, He says: 'Thou shalt not have strange gods other than Me. Thou shalt not make to thyself a graven thing, nor any similitude. Thou shalt not adore them, and thou shalt not serve them, for I am the Lord thy God.' And again, 'Overthrow their altars, and break down their statues; burn their groves with fire, and break their idols in pieces. For thou shalt not adore a strange god.' And a little further on: 'Thou shalt not make to thyself gods of metal.'

You see that He forbids image-making on account of idolatry, and that it is impossible to make an image of the immeasurable, un-circumscribed, invisible God. You have not seen the likeness of Him, the Scripture says, and this was St Paul's testimony as he stood in the midst of the Areopagus: 'Being, therefore, the offspring of God, we must not suppose the divinity to be like unto gold, or silver, or stone, the graving of art, and device of man.'

These injunctions were given to the Jews on account of their proneness to idolatry. Now we, on the contrary, are no longer in leading strings. Speaking theologically, it is given to us to avoid superstitious error, to be with God in the knowledge of the truth, to worship God alone, to enjoy the fulness of His knowledge. We have passed the stage of infancy, and reached the perfection of manhood. We receive our habit of mind from God, and know what may be imaged and what may not. The Scripture says, ' You have not seen the likeness of Him.' What wisdom in the law-giver. How depict the invisible? How picture the inconceivable? How give expression to the limitless, the immeasurable, the invisible? How give a form to immensity? How paint immortality? How localise mystery? It is clear that when you contemplate God, who is a pure spirit, becoming man for your sake, you will be able to clothe Him with the human form. When the Invisible One becomes visible to flesh, you may then draw a likeness of His

form. When He who is a pure spirit, without form or limit, immeasurable in the boundlessness of His own nature, existing as God, takes upon Himself the form of a servant in substance and in stature, and a body of flesh, then you may draw His likeness, and show it to anyone willing to contemplate it. Depict His ineffable condescension, His virginal birth, His baptism in the Jordan, His transfiguration on Thabor, His all-powerful sufferings, His death and miracles, the proofs of His Godhead, the deeds which He worked in the flesh through divine power, His saving Cross, His Sepulchre, and resurrection, and ascent into heaven. Give to it all the endurance of engraving and colour. Have no fear or anxiety; worship is not all of the same kind. Abraham worshipped the sons of Emmor, impious men in ignorance of God, when he bought the double cave for a tomb. Jacob worshipped his brother Esau and Pharao, the Egyptian, but on the point of his staff.*
He worshipped, he did not adore. Josue and Daniel worshipped an angel of God; they did not adore him. The worship of latreia is one thing, and the worship which is given to merit

---

* ἀλλὰ μὴν καὶ ἐπὶ τὸ ἄκρον τῆς ῥάβδου.

another. Now, as we are talking of images and worship, let us analyse the exact meaning of each. An image is a likeness of the original with a certain difference, for it is not an exact reproduction of the original. Thus, the Son is the living, substantial, unchangeable Image of the invisible God, bearing in Himself the whole Father, being in all things equal to Him, differing only in being begotten by the Father, who is the Begetter; the Son is begotten. The Father does not proceed from the Son, but the Son from the Father. It is through the Son, though not after Him, that He is what He is, the Father who generates. In God, too, there are representations and images of His future acts,—that is to say, His counsel from all eternity, which is ever unchangeable. That which is divine is immutable; there is no change in Him, nor shadow of change. Blessed Denis (the Carthusian) who has made divine things in God's presence his study, says that these representations and images are marked out beforehand. In His counsels, God has noted and settled all that He would do, the unchanging future events before they came to pass. In the same way, a man who wished to build a house, would first make and think out a plan. Again, visible things are images of invisible and intangible things, on which they throw a faint light. Holy Scripture clothes in figure God and the angels, and the same holy man (Blessed Denis) explains why. When sensible things sufficiently render what is beyond sense, and give a form to what is intangible, a medium would be reckoned imperfect according to our standard, if it did not fully represent material vision, or if it required effort of mind. If, therefore, Holy Scripture, providing for our need, ever putting before us what is intangible, clothes it in flesh, does it not make an image of what is thus invested with our nature, and brought to the level of our desires, yet invisible? A certain conception through the senses thus takes place in the brain, which was not there before, and is transmitted to the judicial faculty, and added to the mental store. Gregory, who is so eloquent about God, says that the mind which is set upon getting beyond corporeal things, is incapable of doing it. For the invisible things of God since the creation of the world are made visible through images. We see images in creation which remind us faintly of God, as when, for instance, we speak of the holy and adorable Trinity, imaged by the sun, or light, or burning rays, or by a running fountain, or a full river, or by the mind, speech, or the spirit within us, or by a rose tree, or a sprouting flower, or a sweet fragrance.

Again, an image is expressive of something in the future, mystically shadowing forth what is to happen. For instance, the ark represents the image of Our Lady, Mother of God,* so does the staff and the earthen jar. The serpent brings before us Him who vanquished on the Cross the bite of the original serpent; the sea, water, and the cloud the grace of baptism.

Again, things which have taken place are expressed by images for the remembrance either of a wonder, or an honour, or dishonour, or good or evil, to help those who look upon it in after times that we may avoid evils and imitate goodness. It is of two kinds, the written image in books, as when God had the law inscribed on tablets, and when He enjoined that the lives of holy men should be recorded and sensible memorials be preserved in re-

---

* Τὴν ἁγίαν παρθένον καὶ θεοτόκον.

membrance; as, for instance, the earthen jar and the staff in the ark. So now we preserve in writing the images and the good deeds of the past. Either, therefore, take away images altogether and be out of harmony with God who made these regulations, or receive them with the language and in the manner which befits them. In speaking of the manner let us go into the question of worship.

Worship is the symbol of veneration and of honour. Let us understand that there are different degrees of worship. First of all the worship of latreia, which we show to God, who alone by nature is worthy of worship. Then, for the sake of God who is worshipful by nature, we honour His saints and servants, as Josue and Daniel worshipped an angel, and David His holy places, when he says, 'Let us go to the place where His feet have stood.' Again, in His tabernacles, as when all the people of Israel adored in the tent, and standing round the temple in Jerusalem, fixing their gaze upon it from all sides, and worshipping from that day to this, or in the rulers established by Him, as Jacob rendered homage to Esau, his elder brother, and to Pharao, the divinely established ruler. Joseph was worshipped by his brothers. I am aware that worship was based on honour, as in the case of Abraham and the sons of Emmor. Either, then, do away with worship, or receive it altogether according to its proper measure.

Answer me this question. Is there only one God? You answer, 'Yes, there is only one Law-giver.' Why, then, does He command contrary things? The cherubim are not outside of creation; why, then, does He allow cherubim carved by the hand of man to overshadow the mercy-seat? Is it not evident that as it is impossible to make an image of God, who is uncircumscribed and impassible, or of one like to God, creation should not be worshipped as God. He allows the image of the cherubim who are circumscribed,* and prostrate in adoration before the divine throne, to be made, and thus prostrate to overshadow the mercy-seat. It was fitting that the image of the heavenly choirs should overshadow the divine mysteries. Would you say that the ark and staff and mercy-seat were not made? Are

* A reference to the question treated by St Thomas after St John Damascene: *utrum angelus sit in loco.*

they not produced by the hand of man? Are they not due to what you call contemptible matter? What was the tabernacle itself? Was it not an image? Was it not a type and a figure? Hence the holy Apostle's words concerning the observances of the law, 'Who serve unto the example and shadow of heavenly things.' As it was answered to Moses, when he was to finish the tabernacle: 'See' (He says), 'that thou make all things according to the pattern which was shown thee on the Mount.' But the law was not an image. It shrouded the image. In the words of the same Apostle, the law contains the shadow of the goods to come, not the image of those things. For if the law should forbid images, and yet be itself a forerunner of images, what should we say? If the tabernacle was a figure, and the type of a type, why does the law not prohibit image-making? But this is not in the least the case. There is a time for everything.

Of old, God the incorporeal and uncircumscribed was never depicted. Now, however, when God is seen clothed in flesh, and conversing with men, I make an image of the God whom I see. I do not worship matter, I worship the God of matter, who became matter for my sake, and deigned to inhabit matter, who worked out my salvation through matter. I will not cease from honouring that matter which works my salvation. I venerate it, though not as God. How could God be born out of lifeless things? And if God's body is God by union (καθ' ὑπόστασιν), it is immutable. The nature of God remains the same as before, the flesh created in time is quickened by a logical and reasoning soul. I honour all matter besides, and venerate it. Through it, filled, as it were, with a divine power and grace, my salvation has come to me. Was not the thrice happy and thrice blessed wood of the Cross matter? Was not the sacred and holy mountain of Calvary matter? What of the life-giving rock, the Holy Sepulchre, the source of our resurrection: was it not matter? Is not the most holy book of the Gospels matter? Is not the blessed table matter which gives us the Bread of Life? Are not the gold and silver matter, out of which crosses and altar-plate and chalices are made? And before all these things, is not the body and blood of our Lord matter? Either do away with the veneration and worship due to all these things, or submit to the tradition of the Church in the worship of images, honouring God and His friends, and following in this the grace of the Holy Spirit. Do not despise matter, for it is not despicable. Nothing is that which God has made. This is the Manichean heresy. That alone is despicable which does not come from God, but is our own invention, the spontaneous choice of will to disregard the natural law,—that is to say, sin. If, therefore, you dishonour and give up images, because they are produced by matter, consider what the Scripture says: And the Lord spoke to Moses, saying, 'Behold I have called by name Beseleel, the son of Uri, the son of Hur, of the tribe of Juda. And I have filled him with the spirit of God, with wisdom and understanding, and knowledge in all manner of work. To devise whatsoever may be artificially made of gold, and silver, and brass, of marble and precious stones, and variety of wood. And I have given him for his companion, Ooliab, the son of Achisamech, of the tribe of Dan. And I have put wisdom in the heart of every skilful man, that they may make all things which I have commanded thee.'

And again: 'Moses said to all the assembly of the children of Israel: This is the word the Lord hath commanded, saying: Set aside with you first fruits to the Lord. Let every one that is willing and hath a ready heart, offer them to the Lord, gold, and silver, and brass, violet, and purple, and scarlet twice dyed, and fine linen, goat's hair, and ram's skins died red and violet, coloured skins, selim-wood, and oil to maintain lights and to make ointment, and most sweet incense, onyx stones, and precious stones for the adorning of the ephod and the rational. Whosoever of you is wise, let him come, and make that which the Lord hath commanded.' See you here the glorification of matter which you make inglorious. What is more insignificant than goat's hair or colours? Are not scarlet and purple and hyacinth colours? Now, consider the handiwork of man becoming the likeness of the cherubim. How, then, can you make the law a pretence for giving up what it orders? If you invoke it against images, you should keep the Sabbath, and practise circumcision. It is certain that 'if you observe the law, Christ will not profit you. You who are justified in the law, you are fallen from grace.' Israel of old did not see God, but we see the Lord's glory face to face.

We proclaim Him also by our senses on all sides, and we sanctify the noblest sense, which is that of sight. The image is a memorial, just what words are to a listening ear. What a book is to the literate, that an image is to the illiterate. The image speaks to the sight as words to the ear; it brings us understanding. Hence God ordered the ark to be made of imperishable wood, and to be gilded outside and in, and the tablets to be put in it, and the staff and the golden urn containing the manna, for a remembrance of the past and a type of the future. Who can say these were not images and far-sounding heralds? And they did not hang on the walls of the tabernacle; but in sight of all the people who looked towards them, they were brought forward for the worship and adoration of God, who made use of them. It is evident that they were not worshipped for themselves, but that the people were led through them to remember past signs, and to worship the God of wonders. They were images to serve as recollections, not divine, but leading to divine things by divine power.

And God ordered twelve stones to be taken out of the Jordan, and specified why. For he says: 'When your son asks you the meaning of these stones, tell him how the water left the Jordan by the divine command, and how the ark was saved and the whole people.' How, then, shall we not record on image the saving pains and wonders of Christ our Lord, so that when my child asks me, 'What is this?' I may say, that God the Word became man, and that for His sake not Israel alone passed through the Jordan, but all the human race gained their original happiness. Through Him human nature rose from the lowest depths of the earth higher than the skies, and in His Person sat down on the throne His Father had prepared for Him.

But the adversary says: 'Make an image of Christ or of His mother who bore Him (τῆς θεοτόκου), and let that be sufficient.' O what folly this is! On your own showing, you are absolutely against the saints. For if you make an image of Christ and not of the saints, it is evident that you do not disown images, but the honour of the saints. You make statues indeed of Christ as of one glorified, whilst you reject the saints as unworthy of honour, and call truth a falsehood. 'I live,' says the Lord, 'and I will glorify those who glorify Me.' And the divine Apostle: therefore now he is not a servant, but a son. 'And if a son, an heir also through God.' Again, 'If we suffer with Him, that we also may be glorified:' you are not waging war against images, but against the saints. St John, who rested on His breast, says, that we shall be like to Him: just as a man by contact with fire becomes fire, not by nature, but by contact and by burning and by participation, so is it, I apprehend, with the flesh of the Crucified Son of God. That flesh, by participation through union (καθ' ὑπόστασιν) with the divine nature, was unchangeably God, not in virtue of grace from God as was the case with each of the prophets, but by the presence of the Fountain Head Himself. God, the Scripture says, stood in the synagogue of the gods, so that the saints, too, are gods. Holy Gregory takes the words, 'God stands in the midst of the gods,' to mean that He discriminates their several merits. The saints in their lifetime were filled with the Holy Spirit, and when they are no more, His grace abides with their spirits and with their bodies in their tombs, and also with their likenesses and holy images, not by nature, but by grace and divine power.

God charged David to build Him a temple through his son, and to prepare a place of rest. Solomon, in building the temple, made the cherubim, as the book of Kings says. And he encompassed the cherubim with gold, and all the walls in a circle, and he had the cherubim carved, and palms inside and out, in a circle, not from the sides, be it observed. And there were bulls and lions and pomegranates. Is it not more seemly to decorate all the walls of the Lord's house with holy forms and images rather than with beasts and plants? Where is the law declaring 'thou shalt not make any graven image'? But Solomon receiving the gift of wisdom, imaging heaven, made the cherubim, and the likenesses of bulls and lions, which the law forbade. Now if we make a statue of Christ, and likenesses of the saints, does not their being filled with the Holy Ghost increase the piety of our homage? As then the people and the temple were purified in blood and in burnt offerings, so now the Blood of Christ giving testimony under Pontius Pilate, and being Himself the first fruits of the martyrs, the Church is built up on the blood of the saints. Then the signs and forms of lifeless animals figured forth the human tabernacle, the martyrs themselves whom they were preparing for God's abode.

We depict Christ as our King and Lord, and do not deprive Him of His army. The saints constitute the Lord's army. Let the earthly king dismiss his army before he gives up his King and Lord. Let him put off the purple before he takes honour away from his most valiant men who have conquered their passions. For if the saints are heirs of God, and co-heirs of Christ, they will be also partakers of the divine glory of sovereignty. If the friends of God have had a part in the sufferings of Christ, how shall they not receive a share of His glory even on earth? 'I call you not servants,' our Lord says, 'you are my friends.' Should we then deprive them of the honour given to them by the Church? What audacity! What boldness of mind, to fight God and His commands! You, who refuse to worship images, would not worship the Son of

God, the Living Image of the invisible God, and His unchanging form. I worship the image of Christ as the Incarnate God; that of Our Lady (τῆς Θεοτόκου), the Mother of us all, as the Mother of God's Son; that of the saints as the friends of God. They have withstood sin unto blood, and followed Christ in shedding their blood for Him, who shed His blood for them. I put on record the excellencies and the sufferings of those who have walked in His footsteps, that I may sanctify myself, and be fired with the zeal of imitation. St Basil says, 'Honouring the image leads to the prototype.' If you raise churches to the saints of God, raise also their trophies. The temple of old was not built in the name of any man. The death of the just was a cause of tears, not of feasting. A man who touched a corpse was considered unclean, even if the corpse was Moses himself. But now the memories of the saints are kept with rejoicings. The dead body of Jacob was wept over, whilst there is joy over the death of Stephen. Therefore, either give up the solemn commemorations of the saints, which are not according to the old law, or accept images which are also against it, as you say. But it is impossible not to keep with rejoicing the memories of the saints. The Holy Apostles and Fathers are at one in enjoining them. From the time that God the Word became flesh He is as we are in everything except sin, and of our nature, without confusion. He has deified our flesh for ever, and we are in very deed sanctified through His Godhead and the union of His flesh with it. And from the time that God, the Son of God, impassible by reason of His Godhead, chose to suffer voluntarily He wiped out our debt, also paying for us a most full and noble ransom. We are truly free through the sacred blood of the Son pleading for us with the Father. And we are indeed delivered from corruption since He descended into hell to the souls detained there through centuries and gave the captives their freedom, sight to the blind, and chaining the strong one.* He rose in the plenitude of His power, keeping the flesh of immortality which He had taken for us. And since we have been born again of water and the Spirit, we are truly sons and heirs of God. Hence St Paul calls the faithful

* δήσας τὸν ἰσχυρὸν.

holy; hence we do not grieve but rejoice over the death of the saints. We are then no longer under grace, being justified through faith, and knowing the one true God. The just man is not bound by the law. We are not held by the letter of the law, nor do we serve as children, but grown into the perfect estate of man we are fed on solid food, not on that which conduces to idolatry. The law is good as a light shining in a dark place until the day breaks. Your hearts have already been illuminated, the living water of God's knowledge has run over the tempestuous seas of heathendom, and we may all know God. The old creation has passed away, and all things are renovated. The holy Apostle Paul said to St Peter, the chief of the Apostles:* 'If you, being a Jew, live as a heathen and not a Jew, how will you persuade heathens to do as Jews do?' And to the Galatians: 'I will bear witness to every circumcised man that it is salutary to fulfil the whole law.'

Of old they who did not know God, worshipped false gods. But now, knowing God, or rather being known by Him, how can we

* τὴν κορυφαίαν ἀκρότητα τῶν ἀποστόλων.

return to bare and naked rudiments? I have looked upon the human form of God, and my soul has been saved. I gaze upon the image of God, as Jacob did, though in a different way. Jacob sounded the note of the future, seeing with immaterial sight, whilst the image of Him who is visible to flesh is burnt into my soul. The shadow and winding sheet and relics of the apostles cured sickness, and put demons to flight. How, then, shall not the shadow and the statues of the saints be glorified? Either do away with the worship of all matter, or be not an innovator. Do not disturb the boundaries of centuries, put up by your fathers.

It is not in writing only that they have bequeathed to us the tradition of the Church, but also in certain unwritten examples. In the twenty-seventh book of his work, in thirty chapters addressed to Amphilochios concerning the Holy Spirit, St Basil says, 'In the cherished teaching and dogmas of the Church, we hold some things by written documents; others we have received in mystery from the apostolical tradition.' Both are of equal value for the soul's growth. No one will dispute this who has considered even a little the discipline of the Church. For if we neglect unwritten customs, as not having much weight, we bury in oblivion the most pertinent facts connected with the Gospel. These are the great Basil's words. How do we know the Holy place of Calvary, or the Holy Sepulchre? Does it not rest on a tradition handed down from father to son? It is written that our Lord was crucified on Calvary, and buried in a tomb, which Joseph hewed out of the rock; but it is unwritten tradition which identifies these spots, and does more things of the same kind. Whence come the three immersions at baptism, praying with face turned towards the east, and the tradition of the mysteries?* Hence St Paul says, Therefore, brethren, stand fast, and hold the traditions which you have learned either by word, or by our epistle. As, then, so much has been handed down in the Church, and is observed down to the present day, why disparage images?

If you bring forward certain practices, they do not inculpate our worship of images, but the worship of heathens who make them idols. Because heathens do it foolishly, this

---

* τα θεια μυστήρια—the Mass.

is no reason for objecting to our pious practice. If the same magicians and sorcerers use supplication, so does the Church with catechumens; the former invoke devils, but the Church calls upon God against devils. Heathens have raised up images to demons, whom they call gods. Now we have raised them to the one Incarnate God, to His servants and friends, who are proof against the diabolical hosts.

If, again, you object that the great Epiphanius thoroughly rejected images, I would say in the first place the work in question is fictitious and unauthentic. It bears the name of some one who did not write it, which used to be commonly done. Secondly, we know that blessed Athanasius objected to the bodies of saints being put into chests, and that he preferred their burial in the ground, wishing to set at nought the strange custom of the Egyptians, who did not bury their dead under ground, but set them upon beds and couches. Thus, supposing that he really wrote this work, the great Epiphanius, wishing to correct something of the same kind, ordered that images should not be used. The proof that he did not object to images, is to be found in his own church, which is adorned with images to this day. Thirdly, the exception is not a law to the Church, neither does one swallow make summer, as it seems to Gregory the theologian, and to the truth. Neither can one expression overturn the tradition of the whole Church which is spread throughout the world.

Accept, therefore, the teaching of Scripture and spiritual writers. If the Scripture *does* call the idols of heathens silver and gold, and the works of man's hand, it does not forbid the adoration of inanimate things, or man's handiwork, but the adoration of demons.

We have seen that prophets worshipped angels, and men, and kings, and the impious, and even a staff. David says, 'And you adore His footstool.' Isaias, speaking in God's name, says, 'The heavens are my throne, and the earth my footstool.' Now, it is evident to every one that the heavens and the earth are created things. Moses, too, and Aaron with all the people adored the work of hands. St Paul, the golden grasshopper* of the Church, says in his Epistle to the Hebrews, 'But Christ being come, a high priest of the good

---

* τεττιξ.

things to come, by a greater and more perfect tabernacle not made by hand,' that is 'not of this creation.' And, again, ' For Jesus is not entered into the Holies made by hands, the patterns of the true ; but into heaven itself.' Thus the former holy things, the tabernacle, and everything within it, were made by hands, and no one denies that they were adored.

AUTHENTIC TESTIMONY OF ANCIENT FATHERS IN FAVOUR OF IMAGES.

St Denis the Areopagite. From his Letter to Bishop Titus.

Instead of attaching the common conception to images, we should look upon what they symbolise, and not despise the divine mark and character which they portray, as sensible images of mysterious and heavenly visions.

Commentary.—Mark that he cautions us not to despise sacred images.

The Same, ' On the Names of God.'

We have taken the same line. On the one side, through the veiled language of Scripture and the help of oral tradition, intellectual things are understood through sensible ones, and the things above nature by the things that are. Forms are given to what is intangible and without shape, and immaterial perfection is clothed and multiplied in a variety of different symbols.

Commentary.—If it be a good work to clothe with shape and form, according to our standard, that which is formless, shapeless, and without consistency, how shall we not make images to ourselves in the same way of things perceived through form and shape, so that we may bear them in mind, and be moved to imitate what they represent.

The Same, on the 'Ecclesiastical Hierarchy.'

Now, if the substances (οὐσίαι) and orders above us, of which we have already made reverent mention, are without bodies, their hierarchy is intellectual and above sense.

We supply by the variety of sensible symbols the visible order, which is according to our own measure. Those sensible symbols lead us naturally to intellectual conception, to God and His divine attributes. Spiritual minds form their own spiritual conceptions, but we are led to the divine vision by sensible images.

Commentary.—If, then, it be rational that we are led to the divine vision by sensible images, and if Divine Providence mercifully clothes in form and image that which is without either for our benefit, what is there unseemly about imaging, according to our capacity, Him who graciously disguised Himself for us in shape and form?

A tradition has come down to us that Angaros, King of Edessa, was drawn vehemently to divine love by hearing of our Lord,* and that he sent envoys to ask for His likeness. If this were refused, they were ordered to have a likeness painted. Then He, who is all-knowing and all-powerful, is said to have taken a strip of cloth, and pressing it to His face, to have left His likeness upon the cloth, which it retains to this day.

St Basil's Sermon on the Martyr St Barlam, beginning, 'In the first place the death of the saints.'

Arise, you renowned painters of brave deeds, who set forth by your art a faint image of the General. My praise of the laurel-crowned victor is faint compared to the colours of your

* τῇ τοῦ κυρίου πρὸς θεῖον ἐκπυρσευθέντα ἔρωτα ἀκοῇ.

brush. I will give up writing on the excellencies of the martyr whom you have crowned. I rejoice at the victory won to-day by your strength. I contemplate the hand put out to the flames, more powerfully dealt with by you. I see the struggle more clearly depicted on your statue. Let demons be enraged even now, overcome by the martyr's excellencies which you reveal. Let the powerful hand be again outstretched to victory. May Christ our Lord, the supreme Judge of the warfare, appear in picture. To Him be glory for ever and ever. Amen.

From the same, from the Thirty Chapters to Amphilochios, on the Holy Ghost.— Chap. xviii.

The image of the king is also called the king, and there are not two kings in consequence. Neither is power divided, nor is glory distributed. Just as the reigning power over us is one, so is our homage one, not many, and the honour given to the image reaches back to the original. What the image is in the one case as a representation, that the Son is by His humanity, and as in art likeness is according to form, so in the divine and incommensurable nature (ἀσυνθέτος) union is effected in the indwelling Godhead.

Commentary.—If the image of the king is the king, the image of Christ is Christ, and the image of a saint the saint, and if power is not divided nor glory distributed, honouring the image becomes honouring the one who is set forth in image. Devils have feared the saints, and have fled from their shadow. The shadow is an image, and I make an image that I may scare demons. If you say that only intellectual worship befits God, take away all corporeal things, light, and fragrance, prayer itself through the physical voice, the very divine mysteries which are offered through matter, bread, and wine, the oil of chrism, the sign of the Cross, for all this is matter. Take away the Cross, and the sponge of the Crucifixion, and the spear which pierced the life-giving side. Either give up honouring these things as impossible, or do not reject the veneration of images. Matter is endued with a divine power through prayer made to those who are depicted in image. Purple by itself is simple, and so is silk, and the cloak which is made of both. But if the king put it on, the cloak receives honour from the honour due to the wearer. So is it with matter. By itself it is of no account, but if the one presented in image be full of grace, men become partakers of his grace according to their faith. The apostles knew our Lord with their bodily eyes; others knew the apostles, others the martyrs. I, too, desire to see them in the spirit and in the flesh, and to possess a saving remedy as I am a composite being. I see with my eyes, and revere that which represents what I honour, though I do not worship it as God. Now you, perhaps, are superior to me, and are lifted up above bodily things, and being, as it were, not of flesh, you make light of what is visible, but as I am human and clothed with a body, I desire to see and to be corporeally with the saints. Condescend to my humble wish that you may be secure on your heights. God accepts my longing for Him and for His saints. For He rejoices at the praises of His servant, according to the great St Basil in his panegyric of the Forty Martyrs. Listen to the words which he uttered in honour of the martyr St Gordion.

From St Basil's Sermon on St Gordion.

The mere memory of just deeds is a source of spiritual joy to the whole world; people are moved to imitate the holiness of which they hear. The life of holy men is as a light illuminating the way for those who would see it. And again, when we recount the story of holy lives we glorify in the first place the Lord of those servants, and we give praise to the servants on account of their testimony, which is known to us. We rejoice the world through good report.

Commentary.—The remembrance of the saints is thus, you see, a glory to God, praise of the saints, joy and salvation to the whole world. Why, then, would you destroy it? This remembrance is kept by preaching and by images, says the same great St Basil.

The same, on the Martyr St Gordion.

Just as burning follows naturally on fire, and fragrance on sweet ointment, so must good arise from holy actions. For it is no small thing to represent past events according to life. Is it a dim memory of the man's wrestlings which has come down to us, and does not the painter's picture tally with our present conflict? Now, as painters draw images from images, they frequently depart from the original as much as the image itself does, and as we did not see what they represent, there is no little fear that we may injure the truth.

The same, at the end.

The sun fills us with perpetual wonder, though always before us, so the memory of this man is ever fresh.

Commentary.—It is evident that it is fresh through sermon and image.

Testimony of the same, from his Sermon on the Forty Martyrs.

Can the lover of the martyrs have too much of their memory? For the honour shown to the just, our fellow-men, is a testimony to the goodness of our common Lord.

And again :—

Recognise the blessedness of the martyr heartily, that you may be a martyr in will; thus, without persecutor, or fire, or blows, found worthy of the same reward.

Commentary.—How, then, would you dissuade me from honouring the saints, and be envious of my salvation? Listen to what he says a little further on to show that he united the painter's art to oratory.

St Basil.

See, then, that setting them before us in representation, we are making them helpful to the living, exhibiting their holiness to us all as if in a picture.

Commentary.—Do you understand that both image and sermon teach one lesson? He says: 'Let us show them forth in a sermon as if in a picture.' And again: Writers and painters point out the struggles of war; the first by the art of style, the second with their brush, and each induce many to be brave. That which a spoken account presents to the hearing, a silent picture portrays for imitation.

Commentary.—What better proof have we that images are the books of the illiterate, the ever-speaking heralds of honouring the saints, teaching those who gaze upon them without words, and sanctifying the spectacle. I have not many books nor time for study, and I go into a church, the common refuge of souls, my mind wearied with conflicting thoughts. I see before me a beautiful picture and the sight refreshes me, and induces me to glorify God. I marvel at the martyr's endurance, at his reward, and fired with burning zeal, I fall down to adore God through His martyr, and receive a grace of salvation. Have you not heard the same holy father in his homily on the beginning of the Psalms, say that the Holy Spirit, knowing the human race were obstinate and hard to lead, mixed honey with the psalm-singing? What do you say to this? Shall I not perpetuate the martyr's testimony both by word and paint brush? Shall I not embrace with my eyes that which is a wonder to the angels and to the whole world, formidable to the devil, a terror to demons, as the same great Father says? Again, towards the end of his homily on the forty martyrs, he exclaims, 'O sainted band! O sacred fraternity! O invincible army! protectors of the human race, solace of the troubled, hope of your petitioners, most powerful intercessors, light of the world, bloom both intellectual and material of the Churches! The earth has not hidden you from sight, heaven has received you. May its gates be opened to you. The spectacle is worthy of angels and patriarchs, prophets, and just.'

Commentary.—How shall I not desire to see what the angels desire? St Basil's brother, who is one with him in thought, St Gregory of Nyssa, shares his sentiments.

St Gregory of Nyssa, from the 'Structure of Man.'

Supplementary.—Just as in human fashion the image makers of the powerful grasp the character of the form and set forth the royal dignity with the insignia of the purple, and their handiwork is called image or king, so is it with human nature. As it was created to rule over other creations, it was made as an animated type or image, partaking of the original in dignity and name.

The same, Fifth Chapter.

The divine beauty is not set forth either in form or comeliness of design or colouring, but is contemplated in speechless blessedness, according to its virtue. So do painters transfer human forms to canvas through certain colours, laying on suitable and harmonious tints to the picture, so as to transfer the beauty of the original to the likeness.

Commentary.—You see that the divine beauty is not set forth in form or shape, and on this account it cannot be conveyed by an image (οὐκ εἰκονίζεται): it is the human form which is transferred to canvas by the artist's brush. If, therefore, the Son of God became man, taking the form of a servant, and appearing in man's nature, a perfect man, why should His image not be made? If, in common parlance, the king's image is called the king, and the honour shown to the image redounds to the original, as holy Basil says, why should the image not be honoured and worshipped, not as God, but as the image of God Incarnate?

The same, from his Sermon at Constantinople on the Godhead of the Son and of the Spirit, and on Abraham.

Then the father proceeds to bind his son. I have often seen paintings of this touching scene, and could not look at it with dry eyes, art setting it forth so vividly. Isaac is lying before the altar, his legs bound, his hands tied behind his back. The father approaching the victim, clasping his hair with the left hand, stoops over the face so piteously turned towards him, and holds in his right hand the sword, ready to strike. Already the point of the sword is on the body when the divine voice is heard, forbidding the consummation.

Leo,* Bishop of Neapolis in Cyprus. From his book against the Jews, on the Adoration of the Cross, and the Statues of the Saints, and on Relics.

If you, O Jew, reproach me saying that I adore the wood of the Cross as God, why do you not reproach Jacob, who worshipped on the point of his staff (ἐπὶ τό ἄκρον τῆς ῥάβδου)? Now it is evident that he was not worshipping wood. So with us; we are worshipping Christ through the Cross, not the wood of the Cross.

Commentary.—If we adore the Cross, made of whatever wood it may be, how shall we not adore the image of the Crucified?

* A short passage from St John Chrysostom, which follows, is omitted on account of Editor's note: *locus hic mihi non occurrit apud Chrysostomum in Epistolam ad Hebræos.*

From the same.

Abraham worshipped the impious men who sold him the cave, and bent his knee to the ground, yet did not worship them as gods. Jacob praised Pharao, an impious idolator, yet not as God, and he fell down at the feet of Esau, yet did not worship him as God. And again, How does God order us to worship the earth and mountains? 'Exalt the Lord your God and worship Him upon His holy mountain, and adore His footstool,' that is, the earth. For heaven is My throne, He says, and the earth My footstool. How was it that Moses worshipped Jothor, an idolator, and Daniel, Nabuchodonosor? How can you reproach me because I honour those who honour God and show Him service? Tell me, is it not fitting to worship the saints, rather than to throw stones at them as you do? Is it not right to worship them, rather than to attack them, and to fling your benefactors into the mire? If you loved God, you would be ready to honour His servants also. And if the bones of the just are unclean, why were the bones of Jacob and

Joseph brought with all honour from Egypt? How was it that a dead man arose again on touching the bones of Eliseus? If God works wonders through bones, it is evident that He can work them through images, and stones, and many other things, as in the case of Eliseus, who gave his staff to his servant, saying, 'With this go and raise from the dead the son of the Sunamitess.' With his staff Moses chastised Pharao, parted the waters, struck the rock, and drew forth the stream. And Solomon said, 'Blessed is the wood by which justice cometh.' Eliseus took iron out of the Jordan with a piece of wood. And again, the wood is the wood of life, and the wood of Sabec, that is, of remission. Moses humbled the serpent with wood and saved the people. The blossoming rod in the tabernacle confirmed the priesthood of Aaron. Perhaps, O Jew, you will tell me that God prescribed to Moses beforehand all the things of the testimony in the tabernacle. Now, I say to you that Solomon made a great variety of things in the temple in carvings and sculpture, which God had not ordered him to do. Nor did the tabernacle of the testimony contain them, nor the temple which God showed to Ezechiel, nor was Solomon to be blamed in this. He had had these sculptured images made for the glory of God as we do. You, too, had many and varied images and signs in the Old Testament to serve as a reminder of God, if you had not lost them through ingratitude. For instance, the rod of Moses, the tablets of the law, the burning bush, the rock giving forth water, the ark containing the manna, the altar set on fire from above ($\pi\upsilon\rho\epsilon\nu\theta\epsilon o\nu$), the lamina bearing the divine name, the ephod, the tabernacle overshadowed by God. If you had prepared all these things by day and by night, saying, 'Glory be to Thee, O Almighty God, who hast done wonders in Israel through all these things'; if through all these ordinances of the law, carried out of old, you had fallen on your knees to adore God, you would see that worship is given to Him by images.

And further on :—

He who truly loves a friend or the king, and especially his benefactor, if he sees that benefactor's son, or his staff, or his chair, or his crown, or his house, or his servant, he holds them fast in his embrace, and if he honours his benefactor, the king, how much more God. Again I repeat it, would that you had made images according to the law of Moses and the prophets, and that day by day you had worshipped the God of images. Whenever, then, you see Christians adoring the Cross, know that they are adoring the Crucified Christ, not the mere wood.* If, indeed, they honoured wood as wood, they would be bound to worship trees of whatever kind, as you, O Israel, worshipped them of old, saying to the tree and to the stone, 'Thou art my God and didst bring me forth.' We do not speak either to the Cross or to the representations of the saints in this way. They are not our gods, but books which lie open and are venerated in churches in order to remind us of God and to lead us to worship Him. He who honours the martyr

* Compare—
>   Ce n'est ni la pierre ni le bois
>   Que le catholique adore ;
>   Mais c'est le Roi qui mort en croix
>   De Son Sang la croix honore.
>   —*Vie de St François de Sales*, par M. Hamond.

honours God, to whom the martyr bore testimony. He who worships the apostle of Christ worships Him who sent the apostle. He who falls at the feet of Christ's mother most certainly shows honour to her Son. There is no God but one, He who is known and adored in the Trinity.

Commentary. — Who is the faithful interpreter of blessed Epiphanius—Leontius, whose teaching adorned the island of Cyprus, or those who spoke according to their own conceits? Listen to the testimony of Severianus, Bishop of the Gabali.

Severianus, Bishop of the Gabali, on the Dedication of the Cross.

How was it that the image of the enemy gave life to our progenitors? . . .

How was it that the image of the serpent worked salvation to the people in distress? Would it not have been more reasonable to say, 'If any of you be bitten, let him look up to heaven, to God, and he shall be saved, or let him look towards the tabernacle of God'? Passing over this, he set up the image of the Cross alone. Why did Moses do this, who said to the people, 'Thou shalt not make to thyself a graven thing, nor the likeness of anything that is in heaven above, or in the earth beneath, nor of those things that are in the waters under the earth'? However, why do I speak to unworthy people? Tell me, devout servant of God, will you do what is forbidden, and disregard what you are told to do? He who said, 'Thou shalt not make to thyself a graven thing,' condemned the golden calf, and you make a brazen serpent, and this not secretly, but most openly, so that it is known to all. Moses answers, I laid down that commandment in order to root out impiety, and to withdraw the people from all apostasy and idolatry; now, I have the serpent cast for a good purpose—as a figure of the truth. And just as I have put up a tabernacle, and everything in it, and cherubim, the likeness of the invisible powers, over the holy of holies, as a sign and figure of the future, so I have set up a serpent for the salvation of the people, to serve as a preliminary to the image of the Cross, and the redemption contained in it. As a confirmation of this, listen to the Lord saying, 'As Moses exalted the serpent in the desert, so must you exalt the Son of Man, that every one believing in Him may not be lost, but may have eternal life.'

Commentary.—Notice that His commandment not to make any graven thing was given to draw the people from idolatry, to which they were prone, and that the brazen serpent was an image of our Lord's suffering.

Listen to what I am going to say as a proof that images are no new invention. It is an ancient practice well known to the best and foremost of the fathers. Elladios, the disciple of blessed Basil and his successor, says in his Life of Basil that the holy man was standing by the image of Our Lady, on which was painted also the likeness of Mercurius, the renowned martyr. He was standing by it asking for the removal of the impious apostate Julian, and he received this revelation from the statue. He saw the martyr vanish for a time, and then reappear, holding a bloody spear.

Taken word for word from the Life of St John Chrysostom.

Blessed John loved the epistles of St Paul exceedingly. . . . He had an image of the apostle in a place where he was wont to retire now and then on account of his physical weakness, for he outdid nature in watchings and vigils. As he read through St Paul's epistles, he had the image before him, and spoke to the apostle as if he had been present, praising him, and directing all his thoughts to him. . . .

When Proclus had finished speaking, gazing intently at the image of the apostle, and recognising the likeness to the man he had seen, saluting John, he said, pointing to the image: 'Forgive me, father; the man I saw talking to you is very like this statue. In fact, I should say he is the same.'

In the life of St Eupraxia we are told that her Superior showed her the likeness of our Lord.

We read in the life of St Mary of Egypt that she prayed before the statue of Our Lady and besought her intercession, and so obtained leave to enter the Church.*

In all the past array of Christian priests and kings, wise and pious, conspicuous by teaching and example, in so many councils of holy and inspired fathers, how is it that no one has

* A testimony quoted from Sophronius is here suppressed.

pointed out these things? We are not advocating a new faith. The law shall come out of Sion, the Holy Ghost said prophetically, and the word of the Lord from Jerusalem. We do not advocate one thing at one time, and another at another, nor that the faith should become a laughing-stock to those outside. We will not allow the king's commands to overturn the tradition handed down from the fathers. It is not for pious kings to overturn ecclesiastical boundaries. These are not patristic ways. Things done by force are impositions, and do not carry persuasion. A proof of this was given in the 2nd Council of Ephesus, when a decree, which has never been recognised as valid, was enforced by the emperor's hand, and blessed Flavian was put to death. Councils do not belong to kings, as the Lord says: 'Wherever one or two are gathered together in My name, there I am in the midst of them.' Christ did not give to kings the power to bind and to loose, but to the apostles, and to their successors and pastors and teachers. 'If an angel were to teach you a different gospel to what you have received,' St Paul says—but we will be silent about what follows, in the hope of their conversion. And if we find the warning disregarded, which may God avert, we will then add the rest. Let us hope it will not be needed.

If any one should enter a house and should see on the walls a history in painting of Moses and Aaron, perchance he might ask about the people who are walking across the sea as if it were dry land. 'Who are they?' he asks. What would you say? 'Are they not the sons of Israel?' 'Who is dividing the sea with his rod?' Would you not say 'Moses'? So if a man makes an image of Christ crucified, and you are asked who he is, you reply, 'It is Christ our Lord, who became incarnate for us.' Yes, O Lord, we adore all that belongs to Thee, and we take to our hearts Thy Godhead, Thy power and goodness, Thy mercy towards us, Thy condescension and Thy Incarnation. And as men fear touching red-hot iron, not because of the iron but because of the heat, so do we worship Thy flesh, not for the nature of flesh, but through the Godhead united to that flesh according to substance. We worship Thy sufferings. Who has ever known death worshipped, or suffering venerated? Yet we truly worship the physical death of our God and His saving sufferings. We adore Thy image and all that is Thine; Thy servants, Thy friends, and most of all Thy Mother, the Mother of God.

We beseech, therefore, the people of God, the faithful flock, to hold fast to the ecclesiastical traditions. The gradual taking away of what has been handed down to us would be undermining the foundation stones, and would in no short time overthrow the whole structure. May we prove steadfast, unflinching, immovable, founded on the solid Rock which is Christ, to whom be praise, glory, and worship, with the Father and the Holy Ghost, now and for ever. Amen.

PART II.

I CRAVE your indulgence, my readers (δέσποταί μου), and ask you to receive the true statement of one who is an unprofitable servant, the least of all, in the Church of God. I have not been moved to speak by motives of vainglory, God is my witness, but by zeal for the truth. In this alone is my hope of salvation, and with it I trust and pray to go out to meet Christ our Lord, asking that it may be an expiation for my sins. The man who received five talents from his lord, brought other five which he had gained, and the man with two, other two. The man who received one, and buried it, gave it back without interest, and being pronounced a wicked servant, was banished into external darkness. Lest I should suffer in the same way, I obey God's commands, and with the talent of eloquence, which is His gift, I put before the wise among you a treasure table, so that when the Lord comes He may find me rich in souls, a faithful servant, whom He may take into that ineffable joy of His, which is my desire. Give me listening ears and willing hearts. Receive my treatise, and ponder well the force of the arguments. This is the second part of my work on images. Certain children of the Church have urged me to do it because the first part was not sufficiently clear to all. Be indulgent with me on this account, for my obedience.

The wicked serpent of old, Beloved, I mean the devil—is wont to wage war in many ways against man, who is made after God's image, and to work his destruction through opposition. In the very beginning he inspired man with the hope and desire of becoming a god, and through that desire he dragged man down to share the death of the brute creation. He has enticed man also by shameful and brutal pleasures. What a contrast between becoming a god and feeling brutal lust. And again, he led man into infidelity, as the royal ($\theta\epsilon o\pi a\tau\omega\rho$) David says: 'The fool said in his heart there is no God.' At one time he has brought man to worship too many gods, at another not even the true God, sometimes demons, and again, the heavens and the earth, the sun and moon and stars, and the rest of creation, wild beasts and reptiles. It is as bad to refuse due honour where honour is due, as to give it where it is not due. Again, he has taught some to call the uncreated god evil, and has deceived others by making them recognise God, who is good by nature, as the author of evil. Some he has deceived by the misconception of one nature and one substance of the Godhead; some he has induced to honour three natures and three substances; some one substance in our Lord Jesus Christ, the Second Person of the Holy Trinity; some two natures and two substances.

But the truth, taking a middle course, sweeps away these misconceptions and teaches us to acknowledge one God, one nature in three persons (ὑποστάσεσι), the Father, the Son, and the Holy Ghost. Evil is not a being,* but an accident, a certain conception, word, or deed against the law of God, taking

---

* See St Augustine, de Civitate Dei: Nemo igitur quærat efficientem causam malæ voluntatis; non enim est efficiens, sed deficiens, quia nec illa effectio sed defectio (xii. c. vii).

its origin in this conception, speech, or doing, and ending with it. The truth proclaims also that in Christ, the second person of the Holy Trinity, there are two natures and one person. Now, the devil, the enemy of the truth and of man's salvation, in suggesting that images of corruptible man, and of birds and beasts and reptiles, should be made and worshipped as gods, has often led astray not only heathens but the children of Israel. In these days he is eager to trouble the peace of Christ's Church through false and lying tongues, using divine words in favour of what is evil, and striving to disguise his wicked intent, and drawing the unstable away from true and patristic custom. Some have risen up and said that it was wrong to represent and set forth publicly for adoration the saving wounds of Christ, and the combats of the saints against the devil. Who with a knowledge of divine things and a spiritual sense does not perceive in this a deception of the devil? He is unwilling that his shame should be known and that the glory of God and of His saints should be published.

If we made an image of the invisible God,

we should in truth do wrong. For it is impossible to make a statue of one who is without body, invisible, boundless, and formless. Again, if we made statues of men, and held them to be gods, worshipping them as such, we should be most impious. But we do neither. For in making the image of God, who became incarnate and visible on earth, a man amongst men through His unspeakable goodness, taking upon Him shape and form and flesh, we are not misled. We long to see what He was like. As the divine apostle says, We see now in a glass, darkly. The image, too, is a dark glass, according to the denseness of our bodies. The mind, in much travail, cannot rid itself of bodily things. Shame upon you, wicked devil, for grudging us the sight of our Lord's likeness and our sanctification through it. You would not have us gaze at His saving sufferings nor wonder at His condescension, neither contemplate His miracles nor praise His almighty power. You grudge the saints the honour God gives to them. You would not have us see their glory put on record, nor allow us to become imitators of their fortitude and faith. We will not obey your suggestions, wicked and man-hating devil. Listen to me, people of all nations, men, women, and children, all of you who bear the Christian name: If any one preach to you something contrary to what the Catholic Church has received from the holy apostles and fathers and councils, and has kept down to the present day, do not heed him. Do not receive the serpent's counsel, as Eve did, to whom it was death. If an angel or an emperor teaches you anything contrary to what you have received, shut your ears. I have refrained so far from saying, as the holy apostle said, 'Let him be anathema,' in the hope of amendment.

But say those who do not enter into the mind of Scripture, God said, through Moses the law-giver: 'Thou shalt not make to thyself the likeness of any thing that is in heaven above, or in the earth beneath'; and through the prophet David: 'Let them be all confounded that adore graven things, and that glory in their idols,' and many similar passages. Whatever they have quoted from Holy Scripture and the fathers is to the same intent.

Now, what shall we say to these things? What, if not that which God spoke to the Jews, 'Search the Scriptures.'

It is good to examine the Scriptures, but let your mind be enlightened from the search. It is impossible, Beloved, that God should not speak truth. There is one God, one Lawgiver of the old and new dispensation, who spoke of old in many ways to the patriarchs through the prophets, and in these latter times through His only begotten Son. Apply your mind with discernment. It is not I who am speaking. The Holy Ghost declared by the holy apostle St Paul that God spoke of old in many different ways to the patriarchs through the prophets. Note, *in many different ways*. A skilful doctor does not invariably prescribe for all alike, but for each according to his state, taking into consideration climate and complaint, season and age, giving one remedy to a child, another to a grown man, according to his age; one thing to a weak patient, another to a strong; and to each sufferer the right thing for his state and malady: one thing in the summer, another in the winter, another in the spring or autumn, and in each place according to its requirements. So in the same way the good Physician of souls prescribed for those who were still children and inclined to the sickness of idolatry, holding idols to be gods, and worshipping them as such, neglecting the worship of God, and preferring the creature to His glory. He charged them not to do this.

It is impossible to make an image of God, who is a pure spirit, invisible, boundless, having neither form nor circumscription. How can we make an image of what is invisible? 'No man hath seen God at any time; the only-begotten Son who is in the bosom of the Father, He hath declared Him.' And again, 'No one shall see My face and live, saith the Lord.'

That they *did* worship idols there is no doubt from what the Scripture says about the going out of the children of Israel, when Moses went up to Mount Sinai, and persevered in prayer to God. Whilst receiving the law, the ungrateful people rose against Aaron, the priest of God, saying: 'Make us gods who may go before us. For as to Moses, we know not what has befallen him.' Then, when they had looked over the trinkets of their wives, and brought them together, they ate and drank, and were inebriated with wine and madness, and began to make merry, saying in their foolishness, 'These are thy gods, O Israel.' Do you see that they made gods of idols who were demons, and that they worshipped the creature instead of the Creator? As the holy apostle says: 'They changed the glory of the incorruptible God into the likeness of the image of a corruptible man and of birds, and of four-footed beasts, and of creeping things, and served the creature rather than the Creator.' On this account God forbade them to make any graven image, as Moses says in Deuteronomy: 'And the Lord spoke to you from the midst of the fire; you heard the voice of His words, but you saw not any form at all.' And a little further on: 'Keep therefore your souls carefully; you saw not any similitude in the day that the Lord God spoke to you in Horeb, from the midst of the fire, lest perhaps being deceived you might make you a graven similitude or image of male or female, the similitude of any beasts that are upon the earth, or of birds that fly under heaven.' And again: 'Lest perhaps lifting up thy eyes to heaven, thou see the sun and the moon, and all the stars of heaven, and being deceived by error, thou adore and serve them.' You see the one object in view is that the creature should not be worshipped instead of the Creator, and that the worship of latreia should be given to God alone. Thus in every case when he speaks of worship he means latreia. Again: 'Thou shalt not have strange gods in my sight; thou shalt not make to thyself a graven thing nor any likeness.' Again: 'Thou shalt not make to thyself gods of metal.' You see that He forbids image-making on account of idolatry, and that it is impossible to make an image of God, who is a Spirit, invisible, and uncircumscribed. 'You have not seen His likeness,' He says; and St Paul, standing in the midst of the Areopagus, says: 'Being therefore the offspring of God, we must not suppose the divinity to be like unto gold, or silver, or stone, the graving of art, a device of man.'

Listen again that it is so. Thou shalt not make to thyself any brazen thing nor any likeness. These things, he says, they made by God's commandment a hanging of violet, purple, scarlet, and fine twisted linen in the entrance of the tabernacle, and the cherubim in woven work. And they made also the propitiatory, that is, the oracle of the purest gold, and the two cherubim. What will you say to this, O Moses? You say, thou shalt not make to thyself any graven thing nor any likeness, and you yourself fashion cherubim of woven work, and two cherubim of pure gold. Listen to the answer of God's servant Moses: 'You blind and foolish people, mark the force of what is said, and keep your souls carefully. I said that you had seen no likeness on the day when the Lord spoke to you on Mount Horeb, in the midst of the fire, lest you should sin against the law and make for yourselves a brazen likeness: thou shalt not make any image or gods of metal. I never said thou shalt not make the image of cherubim in adoration before the propitiatory. What I said was: Thou shalt not make to thyself gods of metal, and thou shalt not make any likeness as of God, nor shalt thou adore the creature instead of the Creator, nor any creature whatsoever as God, nor have

I served the creature rather than the Creator.'

Note how the object of Scripture becomes clear to those who really search it. You must know, Beloved, that in every business truth and falsehood are distinguished, and the object of the doer, whether it be good or bad. In the gospel we find all things good and evil. God, the angels, man, the heavens, the earth, water and fire and air, the sun and moon and stars, light and darkness, Satan and the devils, the serpent and scorpions, death and hell, virtues and vices. And because everything told about them is true, and the object in view is the glory of God and the saints whom He has honoured, our salvation, and the shame of the devil, we worship and embrace and love these utterances, and receive them with our whole heart as we do the whole of the old and new dispensation, and all the spoken testimony of the holy fathers. Now, we reject the evil, abominable writings of heathens and Manicheans, and all other heretics, as containing foolishness and lies, promoting the advantage of Satan and his demons, and giving them pleasure, although they contain the name of God. So with regard to images we must manifest the truth, and take into account the intention of those who make them. If it be in very deed for the glory of God and of His saints to promote goodness, to avoid evil, and save souls, we should receive and honour and worship them as images, and remembrances, likenesses, and the books of the illiterate. We should love and embrace them with hand and heart as reminders of the incarnate God, or His Mother, or of the saints, the participators in the sufferings and the glory of Christ, the conquerors and overthrowers of Satan, and diabolical fraud. If any one should dare to make an image of Almighty God, who is pure Spirit, invisible, uncircumscribed, we reject it as a falsehood. If any one make images for the honour and worship of the Devil and his angels, we abhor them and deliver them to the flames. Or if any one give divine honours to the statues of men, or birds, or reptiles, or any other created thing, we anathematise him. As our forefathers in the faith pulled down the temples of demons, and erected on the same spot churches dedicated to saints whom we honour, so they overturned the statues of demons, and set up instead the images of Christ, of His holy Mother, and the saints. Even in the old dispensation, Israel neither raised temples to human beings, nor held sacred the memory of man. At that time Adam's race was under a curse, and death was a penalty, therefore a mourning. A corpse was looked upon as unclean, and the man who touched it as contaminated. But since the Godhead has taken to Himself our nature, it has become glorified as a vivifying and efficacious remedy, and has been transformed unto immortality. Thus the death of the saints is a rejoicing, and churches are raised to them, and their images are set up. Be assured that any one wishing to pull down an image erected out of pure zeal for the glory and enduring memory of Christ, or of His holy Mother, or any of the saints, to put the devil and his satellites to shame,—anyone, I say, refusing to honour and worship this image as sacred—it is not to be worshipped as God—is an enemy of Christ, of His blessed Mother, and of the saints, and is an advocate of the devil and his crew, showing grief by his conduct that the saints are honoured and glorified, and the devil put to shame. The image is a hymn of praise, a manifestation, a lasting token of those who have fought and conquered, and of demons humbled and put to flight.

Kings have no call to make laws in the Church. What does the holy apostle say? 'And God, indeed, hath set some in the church, first apostles, secondly prophets, thirdly doctors and shepherds' for the training of the Church. He does not say 'kings.' And again: 'Obey your prelates, and be subject to them. For they watch as being to render an account of your souls.' Again: 'Remember your prelates who have spoken the word of God to you, whose faith follow, considering the end of your conversation.' Kings have not spoken the word to you, but apostles and prophets, pastors and doctors. When God was speaking to David about building a house for Him, He said: 'Thou shalt not build me a house, for thou art a man of blood.' 'Render, therefore, to all men their dues,' St Paul exclaimed; 'tribute to whom tribute is due, custom to whom custom, fear to whom fear, honour to whom honour.' The political prosperity is the king's business : * the ecclesiastical organisation

---

* βασιλέων ἐστὶν ἡ πολιτικὴ εὐπραξία ; ἡ δὲ ἐκκλησιαστικὴ κατάστασις, ποιμένων καὶ διδασκάλων. λῃστρικὴ ἔφοδός ἐστιν αὕτη.

belongs to pastors and doctors, and to take it out of their hands is to commit an act of robbery. Saul rent Samuel's cloak, and what was the consequence? God took from him his royalty, and gave it to the meek David. Jezabel pursued Elias, pigs and dogs licked up her blood, and harlots were bathed in it. Herod removed John, and was consumed by worms. And now holy Germanus, shining by word and example, has been punished and become an exile, and many more bishops and fathers, whose names are unknown to us. Is not this a persecution? When the Pharisees and the learned surrounded our Lord, ostensibly to listen to His teaching, and when they asked Him if it was lawful to pay tribute to Cæsar, He answered them: 'Bring me a coin.' And when they had brought it, He said: 'Whose image is this?' Upon their reply, 'Cæsar's,' He said, 'Give to Cæsar that which is Cæsar's and to God that which is God's.' We are obedient to you, O King, in things concerning our daily life, in tributes, taxes, and payments, which are your due; but in ecclesiastical government we have our pastors, preachers of the word, and exponents of ecclesiastical law.

We do not change the boundaries marked out by our fathers: we keep the tradition we have received. If we begin to lay down the law to the Church, even in the smallest thing, the whole edifice will fall to the ground in no short time.

You look down upon matter and call it contemptible. This is what the Manicheans did, but holy Scripture pronounces it to be good; for it says, 'And God saw all that He had made, and it was very good.' I say matter is God's creation and a good thing. Now, if you say it is bad, you say either that it is not from God, or you make Him a cause of evil. Listen to the words of Scripture concerning matter, which you despise: 'And Moses said to all the assembly of the children of Israel: This is the word the Lord hath commanded, saying: Set aside with you first fruits to the Lord; let every one that is willing and hath a ready heart, offer them to the Lord: gold, and silver, and brass, violet and purple, and scarlet twice dyed, and fine linen, goat's hair, and ram's skins dyed red, and violet, and coloured skins, selimwood, and oil to maintain lights, and to make ointment, and most sweet incense, onyx stones and precious stones for the adorning of the ephod and the rational : Whosoever of you is wise let him come and make that which the Lord hath commanded : to wit, the tabernacle,' etc.

Behold, then, matter is honoured, and you dishonour it. What is more insignificant than goat's hair, or colours, and are not violet and purple and scarlet colours? And the likeness of the cherubim are the work of man's hand, and the tabernacle itself from first to last was an image. 'Look,' said God to Moses, 'and make it according to the pattern that was shown thee in the Mount,' and it was adored by the people of Israel in a circle. And, as to the cherubim, were they not in sight of the people? And did not the people look at the ark, and the lamps, and the table, the golden urn and the staff, and adore? It is not matter which I adore ; it is the Lord of matter, becoming matter for my sake, taking up His abode in matter and working out my salvation through matter. For the Word was made Flesh, and dwelt amongst us. It is evident to all that flesh is matter, and that it is created. I reverence and honour matter, and worship that which has brought about my salvation. I honour it, not as God, but as a channel of divine strength and grace. Was not the thrice blessed wood of the Cross matter? and the sacred and holy mountain of Calvary? Was not the holy sepulchre matter, the life-giving stone the source of our resurrection? Was not the book of the Gospels matter, and the holy table which gives us the bread of life? Are not gold and silver matter, of which crosses, and holy pictures, and chalices are made? And above all, is not the Lord's Body and Blood composed of matter? Either reject the honour and worship of all these things, or conform to ecclesiastical tradition, sanctifying the worship of images in the name of God and of God's friends, and so obeying the grace of the Divine Spirit. If you give up images on account of the law, you should also keep the Sabbath and be circumcised, for these are severely inculcated by it. You should observe all the law, and not celebrate the Lord's Passover out of Jerusalem. But you must know that if you observe the law, Christ will profit you nothing. You are ordered to marry your brother's wife, and so carry on his name, and not to sing the song of the Lord in a strange land. Enough of this!

Those who have been justified by the law have fallen from grace.

Let us set forth Christ, our King and Lord, not depriving Him of His army. The saints are His army. Let the earthly king strip himself of his army, and then of his own dignity. Let him put off the purple and the diadem before he take honour away from his most valiant men who have conquered their passions.* For if the friends of Christ are heirs of God and co-heirs of Christ, and are to be partakers of the divine glory and kingdom, is not even earthly glory due to them? I call you not servants, our Lord says; you are my friends. Shall we, then, withhold from them the honour which the Church gives them? You are a bold and venturesome man to fight against God and His ordinances. If you do not worship images, you do not worship the Son of God, who is the living image of the invisible God, and the immutable figure of His substance. The temple which Solomon built was consecrated by the blood of animals, and

* γυμνώσατω ἑαυτὸν τοῦ οἰκείου στρατεύματος ὁ ἐπίγειος βασιλεὺς, καὶ τότε τὸν ἑαυτοῦ βασιλέα καὶ κύριον. Ἀποθέσθω τὴν ἁλουργίδα καὶ το διάδημα καὶ τότε τῶν κατὰ τοῦ τυράννου ἀριστευσάντων, καὶ βασιλεύσαντων τῶν παθῶν σέβας περιαιρείτω.

decorated by images of lions, oxen, and the palms and pomegranates. Now, the Church is consecrated by the blood of Christ and of His saints, and it is adorned with the image of Christ and of His saints. Either take away the worship of images altogether, or be not an innovator, and pass not beyond the ancient boundaries which thy fathers have set. I am not speaking of boundaries prior to the incarnation of Christ our Lord, but since His coming. God spoke to them, depreciating the traditions of the old law, saying, ' I also gave them statutes that were not good,' on account of their hardness of heart. Consequently on the change of priesthood the law of necessity was also changed.

The eye-witnesses and ministers of the word handed down the teaching of the Church, not only by writing, but also by unwritten tradition. Whence comes our knowledge of the sacred spot, Mount Calvary, of the holy sepulchre? Has it not been handed down to us from father to son? It is written that our Lord was crucified on Calvary, and buried in the tomb which Joseph hewed out of the rock, but it is unwritten tradition that teaches us we are adoring the right places, and many other things of the same kind. Why do we believe in three baptisms, that is, in three immersions? Why do we adore the Cross? Is it not through tradition? Therefore the holy apostle says : 'Brethren, stand fast ; and hold the traditions which you have learned, whether by word, or by our epistle.' Many things, therefore, being handed down to the Church by unwritten tradition and kept up to the present day, why do you speak slightingly of images? The Manicheans followed a gospel according to Thomas, and you will follow that of Leo. I do not admit an emperor's tyrannical action in domineering over the Church. The emperor has not received the power to bind and loose. I know of the Emperor Valens, a Christian in name, who persecuted the true faith, Zeno and Anastasius, Heraclius and Constantine of Sicily, and Bardaniskus, called Philip (φιλιππι κου). I am not to be persuaded that the Church is set in order by imperial edicts, but by patristic traditions, written and unwritten. As the written Gospel has been preached in the whole world, so has it been an unwritten tradition in the whole world to represent in image Christ, the incarnate God, and the saints, to adore the Cross, and to pray towards the east.

The customs which you bring forward do not incriminate our worship of images, but that of the heathens who make idols of them. The pious practice of the Church is not to be rejected because of heathen abuse. Sorcerers and magicians exorcise; the Church exorcises catechumens. The former invoke demons, the Church calls upon God against demons. Heathens sacrificed to demons; Israel offered to God both holocausts and victims. The Church, too, offers an unbloody sacrifice to God. Heathens set up images to demons, and Israel made idols of them in the words, 'These are thy gods, O Israel, who brought thee out of Egypt.' Now we have set up images to the true God incarnate, to His servants and friends, who have put the demon host to flight. If you say to this that blessed Epiphanius clearly rejected our use of images, you must know that the work in question is spurious and written by some one else in the name of Epiphanius, as often happens. A father does not fight his own children. All have become participators in the one Spirit.

The Church is a witness of this in adorning images, until some men rose up against her and disturbed the peace of Christ's fold, putting poisoned food before the people of God.

If I venerate and worship, as the instruments of salvation, the Cross and lance, and reed and sponge, by means of which the Jews (θεοκτονοι) scorned and put to death my Lord, shall I not also worship images that Christians make with a good intention for the glory and remembrance of Christ? If I worship the image of the Cross, made of whatever wood it may be, shall I not worship the image which shows me the Crucified and my salvation through the Cross? Oh, inhumanity of man! It is evident that I do not worship matter, for supposing the Cross, if it be made of wood, should fall to pieces, I should throw them into the fire, and the same with images.

Receive the united testimony of Scripture and the fathers to show you that images and their worship are no new invention, but the ancient tradition of the Church. In the holy Gospel of St Matthew our Lord called His disciples blessed, and with them all those who followed their example and walked in their footsteps in these words: 'Blessed are your eyes, because they see, and your ears, because they hear. For, amen I say to you, many prophets and just men have desired to see the things that you see, and have not seen them, and to hear the things that you hear, and have not heard them.' We also desire to see as much as we may. 'We see now in a glass, darkly,' and in image, and are blessed. God Himself first made an image, and showed forth images. For He made the first man after His own image. And Abraham, Moses, and Isaias, and all the prophets saw images of God, not the substance of God. The burning bush was an image of God's Mother, and as Moses was about to approach it, God said: 'Put off the shoes from thy feet, for the place whereon thou standest is holy ground.' Now if the spot on which Moses saw an image of Our Lady was holy, how much more the image itself? And not only is it holy, but I venture to say it is the holy of holies (ἁγίων ἅγια). When the Pharisees asked our Lord why Moses had allowed a bill of divorce, He answered: 'On account of the hardness of your hearts Moses allowed you to divorce your wife, but in the beginning it was not so.' And I say to you that Moses, through the children of Israel's hardness of heart, and knowing their proclivity to idolatry, forbade them to make images. We are not in the same case. We have taken a firm footing on the rock of faith, being enriched with the light of God's friendship.

Listen to our Lord's words: 'Ye foolish and blind, whosoever shall swear by the temple, sweareth by it, and by him that dwelleth in it; and he that sweareth by heaven sweareth by the throne of God, and by Him that sitteth thereon.' And he who swears by an image swears by the one whom it represents. It has been sufficiently proved that the tabernacle, and the veil, the ark and the table, and everything within the tabernacle, were images and types, and the works of man's hand, which were worshipped by all Israel, and also that the cherubim in carving were made by God's order. For God said to Moses, 'See that thou doest all things according to the pattern shown to thee on the mount.' Listen, too, to the apostle's testimony that Israel worshipped images and the handiwork of man in obedience to God: 'If, then, he were on earth he would not be a priest; seeing that there would be others to offer gifts according to the law, who serve unto the example and shadow of heavenly things, as it was answered to Moses, when he was to finish the tabernacle: See (says he) that thou make all things according to the pattern which was shown thee on the mount. But now he hath obtained a better ministry, by how much also he is a mediator of a better testament, which is established on better promises. For if that former had been faultless, there should not indeed a place have been sought for a second. For finding fault with them, he saith: 'Behold the day shall come, saith the Lord: and I will perfect unto the house of Israel, and unto the house of Juda, a New Testament: not according to the Testament which I made to their fathers, on the day when I took them by the hand to lead them out of the land of Egypt.' And a little further on: 'Now in saying a New, he hath made the former Old. And that which decayeth and groweth old, is near its end. For there was a tabernacle made the first, wherein were the candlesticks, and the table, and the setting forth of loaves, which is called the Holy. And after the second veil, the tabernacle, which is called the Holy of Holies; having a golden censer, and the ark of the testament covered about on every part with gold, in which was a golden pot that had manna, and the rod of Aaron that had blossomed, and the tables of the testament. And over it were the cherubims of glory overshadowing the propitiatory.' And again: 'For Jesus is not entered into the Holies made with hands, the patterns of the true; but into heaven itself.' And again: 'For the law having a shadow of the good things to come, not the very image of the things.'

You see that the law and everything it ordained and all our own worship consist in the consecration of what is made by hands, leading us through matter to the invisible God. Now the law and all its ordinances were a foreshadowing of the image in the future, that is, of our worship. And our worship is an image of the eternal reward. As to the thing itself, the heavenly Jerusalem, it is invisible and immaterial, as the same divine apostle says: 'We have not here an abiding city, but we seek for the one above, the heavenly Jerusalem, of which God is Lord and Architect.' All ordinances of the law and of our worship have been directed for that heavenly city. To God be praise for ever. Amen.

TESTIMONY OF ANCIENT AND LEARNED FATHERS TO IMAGES.*

St John Chrysostom. From His 'Commentary on the Parable of the Sower.'

If you despise the royal garment, do you not despise the king himself? Do you not see that if you despise the image of the king, you despise the original? Do you not know that if a man shows contempt for an image of wood or a statue of metal, he is not judged as if he had vented himself on lifeless matter, but as showing contempt for the king? Dishonour shown to an image of the king is dishonour shown to the king.

The same, from his Sermon to St Meletius, Bishop of Antioch, and on the zeal of his hearers, beginning, 'Casting his eyes everywhere on this holy flock.'

What took place was most edifying, and

---

* The first quotations are only repetitions, and are consequently omitted.

we ought always to bear this consolation in mind, and to have this saint before our eyes, whose name was invoked against every bad passion and specious argument. This was so much the case that streets, market-place, fields, every nook and corner rang with his name. Not only have you longed to invoke him, but to look upon his bodily form. As with his name so with his image. Many people have put it on their rings and goblets and cups and on their bedroom walls, so as not only to hear his history but to look upon his physical likeness, and to have a double consolation in his loss.*

St Maximus, Philosopher and Confessor. From his 'Acts' and those of Bishop Theodosius.

And after this all rose with tears of devotion, and kneeling down, prayed. And every one kissed the holy Gospels, and the sacred Cross, and the image of our Lord and Saviour Jesus Christ, and of Our Lady, His Immaculate Mother (παναγίας θεοτόκου), putting their hands to it in confirmation of what had been said.

* Two slight omissions, viz., St Chrysostom and St Ambrose.

Blessed Anastasius, Archbishop of Theopolis, on the Sabbath, to Simeon, Bishop of Bostris.

As in the king's absence his image is honoured instead of himself, so in his presence it would be unseemly to leave the original for the image. This is not to say that what is passed over in his presence should be dishonoured. . . . As the man who shows disrespect to the king's image is punished as if he had shown it to the king in very deed, although the image is composed merely of wood and paint moulded together, so one who shows disrespect to the likeness of a man means it for the original of the likeness.

PART III.*

EVERY one must recognise that a man who attempts to dishonour an image which has been set up for the glory and remembrance of Christ, of His holy Mother, or one of his saints, is an enemy of Christ, of His holy Mother, and the saints. It is also set up to shame the devil and his crew, out of love and zeal for God. The man who refuses to give this image due, though not divine, honour, is an upholder of the devil and his demon host, showing by his act grief that God and the saints are honoured and glorified, and the devil put to shame. The image is a canticle and manifestation and monument to the memory of those who have fought bravely and won the victory to the shame and confusion of the vanquished. I have often seen lovers gazing at the loved

* A repetition up to ‹ (x), where the translation begins.

one's garment, and embracing it with eyes and mouth as if it was himself. We must give his due to every man. St Paul says : 'Honour to whom honour : to the king as excelling : or to governors as sent by him,' to each according to the measure of his dignity.

Where do you find in the Old Testament or in the Gospel the Trinity, or consubstantiality, or one Godhead, or three persons,* or the one substance of Christ, or His two natures, expressed in so many words? Still, as they are contained in what Scripture *does* say, and defined by the holy fathers, we receive them and anathematise those who do not. I prove to you that in the old law God commanded images to be made, first of all the tabernacle and everything in it. Then in the gospel our Lord Himself said to those who asked Him, tempting, whether it was lawful to give tribute to Cæsar, 'Bring me a coin, and they showed Him a penny. And He asked them whose likeness it was, and they said to Him, Cæsar's; and He said, 'Give to Cæsar that which is Cæsar's, and to God that which is God's.' As the coin bears the likeness of Cæsar, it is his,

* τρεις ὑποστασεις.

and you should give it to Cæsar. So the image bears the likeness of Christ, and you should give it Him, for it is His.

Our Lord called His disciples blessed, saying, 'Many kings and prophets have desired to see what you see, and have not seen it, and to hear what you hear and have not heard it. Blessed are your eyes which see and your ears which hear.' The apostles saw Christ with their bodily eyes, and His sufferings and wonders, and they listened to His words. We, too, desire to see, and to hear, and to be blessed. They saw Him face to face, as He was present in the body. Now, since he is not present in the body to us, we hear His words from books and are sanctified in spirit by the hearing, and are blessed, and we adore, honouring the books which tell us of His words. So, through the representation of images, we look upon His bodily form, and upon His miracles and His sufferings, and are sanctified and satiated, gladdened and blessed. Reverently we worship His bodily form, and contemplating it, we form some notion of His divine glory. For, as we are composed of soul and body, and our soul does not stand alone, but is, as it were, shrouded by a veil, it is impossible for us to arrive at intellectual conceptions without corporeal things. Just as we listen with our bodily ears to physical words and understand spiritual things, so, through corporeal vision, we come to the spiritual. On this account Christ took a body and a soul, as man has both one and the other. And baptism likewise is double, of water and the spirit. So is communion and prayer and psalmody; everything has a double signification, a corporeal and a spiritual. Thus again, with lights and incense. The devil has tolerated all these things, raising a storm against images alone. His great jealousy of them may be learnt by what St Sophronius, Patriarch of Jerusalem, recounts in his 'Spiritual Garden.' Abbot Theodore Æliotes told of a holy hermit on the Mount of Olives, who was much troubled by the demon of fornication. One day when he was sorely tempted, the old man began to complain bitterly. 'When will you let me alone?' he said to the devil: 'begone from me! you and I have grown old together.' The devil appeared to him, saying,

'Swear to me that you will keep what I am about to tell you to yourself, and I will not trouble you any longer.' And the old man swore it. Then the devil said to him, ' Do not worship this image, and I will not harass you.' The image in question represented Our Lady, the holy Mother of God, bearing in her arms our Lord Jesus Christ. You see what those who forbid the worship of images hate in reality, and whose instruments they are. The demon of fornication strove to prevent the worship of Our Lady's image rather than to tempt the old man to impurity. He knew that the former evil was greater than fornication.

As we are treating of images and their worship, let us draw out the meaning more accurately and say in the first place what an image is; (2) Why the image was made; (3) How many kinds of images there are; (4) What may be expressed by an image, and what may not; (5) Who first made images. Again, as to worship : (1) What is worship; (2) How many kinds of worship there are; (3) What are the things worshipped in Scripture; (4) That all worship is for God, who is worshipful by nature; (5) That honour shown to the image is given to the original.

1st Point.—What is an Image?

An image is a likeness and representation of some one, containing in itself the person who is imaged. The image is not wont to be an exact reproduction of the original. The image is one thing, the person represented another; a difference is generally perceptible, because the subject of each is the same. For instance, the image of a man may give his bodily form, but not his mental powers. It has no life, nor does it speak or feel or move. A son being the natural image of his father is somewhat different from him, for he is a son, not a father.

2nd Point.—For what purpose the Image is made.

Every image is a revelation and representation of something hidden. For instance, man has not a clear knowledge of what is invisible, the spirit being veiled to the body, nor of future things, nor of things apart and distant, because he is circumscribed by place and time.

The image was devised for greater knowledge, and for the manifestation and popularising of secret things, as a pure benefit and help to salvation, so that by showing things and making them known, we may arrive at the hidden ones, desire and emulate what is good, shun and hate what is evil.

3rd Point.—How many kinds of Images there are.

Images are of various kinds. First there is the natural image. In everything the natural conception must be the first, then we come to institution according to imitation. The Son is the first natural and unchangeable image of the invisible God, the Father, showing the Father in Himself. 'For no man has seen God.' Again, 'Not that any one has seen the Father.' The apostle says that the Son is the image of the Father, 'Who is the image of the invisible God,' and to the Hebrews, 'Who being the brightness of His glory, and the figure of His substance.' In the Gospel of St John we find that He *does* show the Father in Himself. When Philip said to Him, 'Show us the Father and it is enough for us,' our Lord replied, 'Have I been so long with you and have you not known Me, Philip? He who sees Me, sees the Father.' For the Son is the natural image of the Father, unchangeable, in everything like to the Father, except that He is begotten, and that He is not the Father. The Father begets, being unbegotten. The Son is begotten, and is not the Father, and the Holy Spirit is the image of the Son. For no one can say the Lord Jesus, except in the Holy Spirit. Through the Holy Spirit we know Christ, the Son of God and God, and in the Son we look upon the Father. For in things that are conceived by nature,* language is the interpreter, and spirit is the interpreter of language. The Holy Spirit is the perfect and unchangeable image of the Son, differing only in His procession. The Son is begotten, but does not proceed. And the son of any father is his natural image. Thus, the natural is the first kind of image.

The second kind of image is that foreknowledge which is in God's mind concerning future events, His eternal and unchanging counsel. God is immutable and His counsel

---

* φύσει γαρ νοούμενα.

without beginning, and as it has been determined from all eternity, it is carried out at the time preordained by Him. Images and figures of what He is to do in the future, the distinct determination of each, are called pre-determinations by holy Dionysius. In His counsels the things predetermined by Him were characterised and imaged and immutably fixed before they took place.

The third sort of image is that by imitation (κατὰ μίμησιν) which God made, that is, man. For how can what is created be of the same nature as what is uncreated, except by imitation? As mind, the Father, the Word, the Son, and the Holy Spirit are one God, so mind and word and spirit are one man, according to God's will and sovereign rule.

For God says: ' Let us make man according to our own image and likeness,' and He adds, 'and let him have dominion over the fishes of the sea and the birds of the air, and the whole earth, and rule over it.'

The fourth kind of image are the figures and types set forth by Scripture of invisible and immaterial things in bodily form, for a clearer apprehension of God and the angels, through our incapacity of perceiving immaterial things unless clothed in analogical material form, as Dionysius the Areopagite says, a man skilled in divine things. Anyone would say that our incapacity for reaching the contemplation of intellectual things, and our need of familiar and cognate mediums, make it necessary that immaterial things should be clothed in form and shape. If, then, holy Scripture adapts itself to us in seeking to elevate us above sense, does it not make images of what it clothes in our own medium, and bring within our reach that which we desire but are unable to see? The spiritual* writer, Gregory, says that the mind striving to banish corporeal images reduces itself to incapability. But from the creation of the world the invisible things of God are made clear by the visible creation. We see images in created things, which remind us faintly of divine tokens. For instance, sun and light and brightness, the running waters of a perennial fountain, our own mind and language and spirit, the sweet fragrance of a flowering rose-tree, are images of the Holy and Eternal Trinity.

* θεορρήμων.

The fifth kind of image is that which is typical of the future, as the bush and the fleece, the rod and the urn, foreshadowing the Virginal Mother of God, and the serpent healing through the Cross those bitten by the serpent of old. Thus, again, the sea, and water and the cloud foreshadow the grace of baptism.

The sixth kind of image is for a remembrance of past events, of a miracle or a good deed, for the honour and glory and abiding memory of the most virtuous, or for the shame and terror of the wicked, for the benefit of succeeding generations who contemplate it, so that we may shun evil and do good. This image is of two kinds, either through the written word in books, for the word represents the thing, as when God ordered the law to be written on tablets, and the lives of God-fearing men to be recorded, or through a visible object, as when He commanded the urn and rod to be placed in the ark for a lasting memory, and the names of the tribes to be engraved on the stones of the humeral. And also He commanded the twelve stones to be taken from the Jordan as a sacred token. Consider the prodigy, the greatest which befel the faithful people, the taking of the ark, and the parting of the waters. So now we set up the images of valiant men for an example and a remembrance to ourselves. Therefore, either reject all images, and be in opposition to Him who ordered these things, or receive each and all with becoming greeting and manner.

Fourth Chapter. What an Image is, what it is not; and how each Image is to be set forth.

Bodies as having form and shape and colour, may properly be represented in image. Now if nothing physical or material may be attributed to an angel, a spirit, and a devil, yet they may be depicted and circumscribed after their own nature. Being intellectual beings, they are believed to be present and to energise in places known to us intellectually. They are represented materially as Moses made an image of the cherubim who were looked upon by those worthy of the honour, the material image offering them an immaterial and intellectual sight. Only the divine nature is uncircumscribed and incapable of being represented in form or shape, and incomprehensible.

If Holy Scripture clothes God in figures which are apparently material, and can even be seen, they are still immaterial. They were seen by the prophets and those to whom they were revealed, not with bodily but with intellectual eyes. They were not seen by all. In a word it may be said that we can make images of all the forms which we see. We apprehend these as if they were seen. If at times we understand types from reasoning, and also from what we see, and arrive at their comprehension in this way, so with every sense, from what we have smelt, or tasted, or touched, we arrive at apprehension by bringing our reason to bear upon our experience.

We know that it is impossible to look upon God, or a spirit, or a demon, as they are. They are seen in a certain form, divine providence clothing in type and figure what is without substance or material being, for our instruction, and more intimate knowledge, lest we should be in too great ignorance of God, and of the spirit world. For God is a pure Spirit by His nature. The angel, and a soul, and a demon, compared to God, who alone is incomparable, are bodies; but compared to material bodies, they are bodiless. God therefore, not wishing that we should be in ignorance of spirits, clothed them in type and figure, and in images akin to our nature, material forms visible to the mind in mental vision. These we put into form and shape, for how were the cherubim represented and described in image? But Scripture offers forms and images even of God.

Who first made an Image.

In the beginning God begot His only begotten Son, His word, the living image of Himself, the natural and unchangeable image of His eternity. And He made man after His own image and likeness. And Adam saw God, and heard the sound of His feet as He walked at even, and he hid in paradise. And Jacob saw and struggled with God. It is evident that God appeared to him in the form of a man. And Moses saw Him, and Isaias saw as it were the back of a man, and as a man seated on a throne. And Daniel saw the likeness of a man, and as the Son of Man coming to the ancient of days. No one saw the nature of God, but the type and image of what was to be. For the Son and Word of the invisible God, was to become man in truth, that He might be united to our nature, and be seen upon earth. Now all who looked upon the type and image of the future, worshipped it, as St Paul says in his epistle to the Hebrews: 'All these died according to faith, not having received the promises, but beholding them afar off, and saluting them.' Shall I not make an image of Him who took the nature of flesh for me? Shall I not reverence and worship Him, through the honour and worship of His image? Abraham saw not the nature of God, for no man ever saw God, but the image of God, and falling down he adored. Josue saw the image of an angel, not as he is, for an angel is not visible to bodily eyes, and falling down he adored, and so did Daniel. Yet an angel is a creature, and servant, and minister of God, not God. And he worshipped the angel not as God, but as God's ministering spirit. And shall not I make images of Christ's friends? And shall I not worship them as the images of God's friends, not as gods? Neither Josue nor Daniel worshipped the angels they saw as gods. Neither do I worship the image as God, but through the image of the saints too, show my worship to God, because I honour His friends, and do them reverence. God did not unite Himself to the angelic nature, but to the human. He did not become an angel: He became a man in nature, and in truth. It is indeed Abraham's seed which He embraces, not the angel's.

The Son of God in person did not take the nature of the angels: He took the nature of man. The angels did not participate in the divine nature, but in working and in grace. Now, men *do* participate, and become partakers of the divine nature when they receive the holy Body of Christ and drink His Blood. For He is united in person to the Godhead,* and two natures in the Body of Christ shared by us are united indissolubly in person, and we partake of the two natures, of the body bodily, and of the Godhead in spirit, or, rather, of each in both. We are made one, not in person, for first we have a person and then we are

---

* θεότητι γὰρ καθ' ὑπόστασιν ἥνωται, καὶ δύο φύσεις ἐν τῷ μεταλαμβανομένῳ ὑφ' ἡμῶν σώματι τοῦ χριστοῦ, ἡνωμεναι καθ' ὑπόστασιν εἰσιν ἀδιασπάστως, καὶ τῶν δύο φύσεων μετέχομεν, τοῦ σώματος, σωματικῶς, τῆς θεότητος, πνευματικῶς·μᾶλλον δὴ ἀμφοῖν κατ' ἄμφω·οὐ καθ' ὑπόστασιν ταυτιζόμενοι·ὑφιστάμεθα γὰρ προτον, καὶ τότε ἑνούμεθα· ἀλλὰ κατα συνανάκρασιν τοῦ σώματος καὶ αἵματος.

united by blending together the body and the blood. How are we not greater than the angels, if through fidelity to the commandments we keep this perfect union? In itself our nature is far removed from the angels, on account of death and the heaviness of the body, but through God's goodness and its union with Him it has become higher than the angels. For angels stand by that nature with fear and trembling, as, in the person of Christ, it sits upon a throne of glory, and they will stand by in trembling at the judgment. According to Scripture they are not partakers of the divine glory. For they are all ministering spirits, being sent to minister because of those who are to be heirs of salvation, not that they shall reign together, nor that they shall be together glorified, nor that they shall sit at the table of the Father. The saints, on the contrary, are the children of God, the children of the kingdom, heirs of God, and co-heirs of Christ. Therefore, I honour the saints, and glorify the servants and friends and co-heirs of Christ: servants by nature, friends by their choice: friends and co-heirs by divine grace, as our Lord said in speaking to the Father.

As we are speaking of images, let us speak of worship also, and in the first place determine what it is.

On Adoration. What is Adoration?

Adoration is a token of subjection,—that is, of submission and humiliation. There are many kinds of adoration.

On the kinds of Adoration.

The first kind is the worship of latreia, which we give to God, who alone is adorable by nature, and this worship is shown in several ways, and first by the worship of servants. All created things worship Him, as servants their master. All things serve Thee, the psalm says. Some serve willingly, others unwillingly; some with full knowledge, willingly, as in the case of the devout, others knowing, but not willing, against their will, as the devil's. Others, again, not knowing the true God, worship in spite of themselves Him whom they do not know.

The second kind is the worship of admiration and desire which we give to God on account of His essential glory. He alone is worthy of praise, who receives it from no one, being Himself the cause of all glory and all good,

He is light, incomprehensible sweetness, incomparable, immeasurable perfection, an ocean of goodness, boundless wisdom, and power, who alone is worthy of Himself to excite admiration, to be worshipped, glorified, and desired.

The third kind of worship is that of thanksgiving for the goods we have received. We must thank God for all created things, and show Him perpetual worship, as from Him and through Him all creation takes its being and subsists. He gives lavishly of His gifts to all, and without being asked. He wishes all to be saved, and to partake of His goodness. He is long-suffering with us sinners. He allows His sun to shine upon the just and unjust, and His rain to fall upon the wicked and the good alike. And being the Son of God, He became one of us for our sakes, and made us partakers of His divine nature, so that we shall be like unto Him, as St John says in his Catholic epistle.

The fourth kind is suggested by the need and hope of benefits. Recognising that without Him we can neither do nor possess anything good, we worship Him, asking Him to satisfy our needs and desires, that we may be preserved from evil and arrive at good.

The fifth kind is the worship of contrition and confession. As sinners we worship God, and prostrate ourselves before Him, needing His forgiveness, as it becomes servants. This happens in three ways. A man may be sorry out of love, or lest he should lose God's benefits, or for fear of chastisement. The first is prompted by goodness and desire for God himself, and the condition of a son : the second is interested, the third is slavish.

What we find worshipped in Scripture, and in how many ways we show worship to creatures.

First, those places in which God, who alone is holy, has rested, and His resting-place in the saints, as in the holy Mother of God and in all the saints. These are they who are made like to God as far as possible, of their own free will, and by God's indwelling, and by His abiding grace. They are truly called gods, not by nature, but by participation ; just as red-hot iron is called fire, not by nature, but by participation in the fire's action. He says :

'Be ye holy because I am holy.' The first thing is the free choice of the will. Then, in the case of a good choice, God helps it on and confirms it. 'I will take up my abode in them,' He says. 'We are the temples of God, and the Spirit of God dwells in us.' Again, He gave them power over unclean spirits, to cast them out, and to heal all manner of diseases, and all manner of infirmities. And again, 'That which I do you shall do, and greater things.' Again: 'As I live,' God says, 'whosoever shall glorify Me, him will I glorify.' Again: If we suffer with Him that we may be also glorified with Him. And 'God stood' in the synagogue of the gods; in the midst of it He points out the gods. As, then, they are truly gods, not by nature, but as partakers of God's nature, so they are to be worshipped, not as worshipful on their own account, but as possessing in themselves Him who *is* worshipful by nature. Just in the same way iron when ignited is not by nature hot and burning to the touch, it is the fire which makes it so. They are worshipped as exalted by God, as through Him inspiring fear to His enemies, and becoming benefactors to the faithful. It is love of God which gives them their free access to Him, not as gods or benefactors by nature, but as servants and ministers of God. We worship them, then, as the king is honoured through the honour given to a loved servant. He is honoured as a minister in attendance upon his master—as a valued friend, not as king. The prayers of those who approach with faith are heard, whether through the servant's intercession with the king, or whether through the king's acceptance of the honour and faith shown by the servant's petitioner, for it was in his name that the petition was made. Thus, those who approached through the apostles obtained their cures. Thus the shadow, and winding-sheets, and girdles of the apostles worked healings. Those who perversely and profanely wish them to be adored as gods are themselves damnable, and deserve eternal fire. And those who in the false pride of their hearts disdain to worship God's servants are convicted of impiety towards God. The children who derided and laughed to scorn Elisseus bear witness to this, inasmuch as they were devoured by bears.

Secondly, we worship creatures by honouring those places or persons whom God has associated with the work of our salvation, whether before our Lord's coming or since the dispensation of His incarnation. For instance, I venerate Mount Sinai, Nazareth, the stable at Bethlehem, and the cave, the sacred mount of Golgotha, the wood of the Cross, the nails and sponge and reed, the sacred and saving lance, the dress and tunic, the linen cloths, the swathing clothes, the holy tomb, the source of our resurrection, the sepulchre, the holy mountain of Sion and the mountain of Olives, the Pool of Bethsaida and the sacred garden of Gethsemane, and all similar spots. I cherish them and every holy temple of God, and everything connected with God's name, not on their own account, but because they show forth the divine power, and through them and in them it pleased God to bring about our salvation. I venerate and worship angels and men, and all matter participating in divine power and ministering to our salvation through it. I do not worship the Jews. They are not participators in divine power, nor have they contributed to my salvation. They crucified my God, the King of

Glory, moved rather by envy and hatred against God their Benefactor. 'Lord, I have loved the beauty of Thy house,' says David, 'we will adore in the place where His feet stood. And adore at His holy mountain.' The holy Mother of God is the living holy mountain of God. The apostles are the teaching mountains of God. 'The mountains skipped like rams, and the hills like the lambs of the flock.'

The third kind of worship is directed to objects dedicated to God, as, for instance, the holy Gospels and other sacred books. They were written for our instruction who live in these latter days. Sacred vessels, again, chalices, thuribles, candelabra, and altars (τραπεζαι) belong to this category. It is evident that respect is due to them all. Consider how Baltassar made the people use the sacred vessels, and how God took away his kingdom from him.

The fourth kind of worship is that of images seen by the prophets. They saw God in sensible vision, and images of future things, as Aaron's rod, the figure of Our Lady's virginity, the urn, and the table. And Jacob worshipped on the point (ἐπὶ τὸ ἄκρον) of his rod. He was a type of our Lord. Images of past events recall their remembrance. The tabernacle was an image of the whole world. 'See,' God said to Moses, 'the type which was shown to thee on the mountain, and the golden cherubim, the work of sculpturers, and the cherubim within the veil of woven work.' Thus we adore the sacred figure of the Cross, the likeness of our God's bodily features, the likeness of her who bore Him, and all belonging to Him.

The fifth manner is in the worship of each other as having upon us the mark of God and being made after His image, humbling ourselves mutually, and so fulfilling the law of charity.

The sixth manner is the worship of those in power who have authority. 'Give to all men their dues,' the apostle says; 'give honour where it is due.' This Jacob did in worshipping Esau as his elder brother, and Pharao the ruler established by God.

In the seventh place, the worship of servants towards their masters and benefactors, and of petitioners towards those who grant their favours, as in the case of Abraham when he bought the double cave from the sons of Emmor.

It is needless to say that fear, desire, and honour are tokens of worship, as also submission and humiliation. No one should be worshipped as God except the one true God. Whatever is due to all the rest is for God's sake.

You see what great strength and divine zeal are given to those who venerate the images of the saints with faith and a pure conscience. Therefore, brethren, let us take our stand on the rock of the faith, and on the tradition of the Church, neither removing the boundaries laid down by our holy fathers of old, nor listening to those who would introduce innovation and destroy the economy of the holy Catholic and Apostolic Church of God. If any man is to have his foolish way, in a short time the whole organisation of the Church will be reduced to nothing. Brethren and beloved children of the Church do not put your mother to shame, do not rend her to pieces. Receive her teaching through me. Listen to what God says of her: 'Thou art all fair, O my love, and there is not a spot in thee.' Let us worship and adore our

God and Creator as alone worthy of worship by nature, and let us worship the holy Mother of God, not as God, but as God's Mother according to the flesh. Let us worship the saints also, as the chosen friends of God, and as possessing access to Him. If men worship kings subject to corruption, who are often bad and impious, and those ruling or deputed in their name, as the holy apostle says, 'Be subject to princes and powers,' and again, 'Give to all their due, to one honour, to another fear,' and our Lord, 'Give to Cæsar that which is Cæsar's, and to God that which is God's,' how much more should we worship the King of Kings? He alone is God by nature; and we should worship His servants and friends who reign over their passions and are constituted rulers of the whole earth. 'Thou shalt make them princes over all the earth,' says David. They receive power against demons and against disease, and with Christ they reign over an incorruptible and unchangeable kingdom. Their shadow alone has put forth disease and demons. Should we not deem a shadow a slighter and weaker thing than an image? Yet it is a true outline of the original. Brethren, the Christian is faith.* He who walks by faith gains many things. The doubter, on the contrary, is as a wave of the sea torn and tossed; he profits nothing. All the saints pleased God by faith. Let us then receive the teaching of the Church in simplicity of heart without questioning. God made man sane and sound. It was man who was over curious. Let us not seek to learn a new faith, destructive of ancient tradition, St Paul says, 'If a man teach any other Gospel than what he has been taught, let him be anathema.' Thus, we worship images, and it is not a worship of matter, but of those whom matter represents. The honour given to the image is referred to the original, as holy Basil rightly says.

And may Christ fill you with the joy of His resurrection, most holy flock of Christ, Christian people, chosen race, body of the Church, and make you worthy to walk in the footsteps of the saints, of the shepherds and teachers of the Church, leading you to enjoy His glory in the brightness of the saints. May you gain His glory for eternity, with the

* Ἀδελφοί, ὁ χριστιανὸς, πίστις ἐστίν.

Uncreated Father, to whom be praise for ever. Amen.

Speaking on the distinction between images and idols, and defining what images are, it is time to give proofs in question, according to our promise.*

* A few Testimonies have been suppressed as unsuitable or irrelevant, viz. :—
 1. St Basil on St Barlaam (in order) 2.
 2. St Gregory of Nyssa. On Isaac and Abraham (5) *Repetition*.
 3. Severianus on the Cross (7) *Repetition*.
 4. From Life of St Chrysostom (8) *Repetition*.
 5. Eusebius on the Woman with an Issue of Blood (22).
 6. Eusebius on Constantine (23).
 7. St Gregory Nazianzen, from his Discourse to Julian the Apostle (2 lines) (24).
 8. St Chrysostom, Commentary on Job (25).
 9. St Chrysostom on Constantine, four quotations (26).
 10. Theodoret of Syrus on Ezechiel (27)
 11. From the Acts of St Placid (28).
 12. Ecclesiastical History of Theodoret (35).
 13. St Athanasius of Mount Sinai (36).
 14. Arcadius, Abp. of Cyprus, on Simeon the Wonderworker (37).
 15. St Chrysostom, Homily (38).
 16. Theodoret, Ecclesiastical History: six short quotations (39).
 17. St Chrysostom on St Flavian and Homily (40).
 18. St Basil on Forty Martyrs, *Repetition* (41).

Testimony of Ancient and Learned Fathers concerning Images.

St Denis, Bishop of Athens, from his letter to St John the Apostle and Evangelist.

Sensible images do indeed show forth invisible things.

The same, from his Homily on the Ecclesiastical Hierarchy.

The substances and orders to which we have already alluded with reverence, are spirits, and they are set forth in spiritual and immaterial array. We can see it when brought down to

19. St Gregory Nazianzen, ex Carminibus (42).
20. St Chrysostom, Commentary on St Paul (43).
21. From the Sixth General Council (44).
22. St Clement, Stromata (45).
23. St Theodore, Bishop of Pentapolis (46).
24. St Basil to St Flavian (51).
25. St Gregory Nazianzen on Baptism (52).
26. St Isidore the Deacon, Chronography (57).
27. From the Fifth General Council (62).
28. Theodore, Ecclesiastical History (63).
29. Abbot Maximus. *Repetition* (64).
30. St Sophronius, Acts of SS. Cyrus and John (65).
31. From the Life of St Eupraxia (69).
32. On the Fifth General Council (70).

our medium, symbolised in various forms, by which we are led up to the mental contemplation of God and divine goodness. Spirits think of Him as spirits according to their nature, but we are led as far as may be by sensible images to the divine contemplation.

Commentary.—If, then, we are led by the medium of sensible images to divine contemplation, what unseemliness is there in making an image of Him Who was seen in the form, and habit, and nature of man for our sakes?

St Basil, from his Homily on the Forty Martyrs.

The fortunes of war are wont to supply matter both for orators and painters. Orators describe them in glowing language, painters depict them on their canvas, and both have led many on to deeds of fortitude. That which words are to the ear, that the silent picture points out for imitation.

The same, on the Thirty Chapters on the Holy Ghost to Amphilochios, 18th Answer.

The image of the king is also called the king, and there are not two kings. Neither power is broken, nor is glory divided. As we are ruled by one government and authority, so our homage is one, not many. Thus the honour given to the image is referred to the original. That which the image represents by imitation on earth, that the Son is by nature in Heaven.

Commentary.—Just, then, as he who does not honour the Son does not honour the Father who sent Him, as our Lord says, so he who does not honour the image does not honour the original. Still some one says, 'We cannot refuse to honour the image of Christ, but we will not have the saints.' What folly! Listen to what our Lord says to His disciples: 'He who receives you receives Me,' so that the man who does not honour the saints does not honour Christ either.

St John Chrysostom, from his 'Commentary on the Epistle to the Hebrews.'

How can what precedes be an image of what follows, as, for instance, Melchisedech of Christ? Just in the same way as a sketch would be an outline of the picture. On this account the old law is called a shadow, and the new—the truth and what is to come—certainties. Thus

Melchisedech, who represents the law, is a foreshadowing of the picture. The new dispensation is the truth; the picture fully completed shows forth eternity. We might call the old dispensation a type of a type, and the new a type of the things themselves.

From the Spiritual History of Theodore, Bishop of Cyrus. From the 'Life of St Simon Stylites.'

It is superfluous to speak of Italy. They say that this man became so well known in the great city of Rome, that small statues were erected to him in all the porticos of workshops, as a certain protection to them, and a guarantee of security.

St Basil, from his 'Commentary on Isaias.'

When the devil saw man made after God's image and likeness, as he could not fight against God, he vented his wickedness on the image of God. In the same way an angry man might stone the King's image, because he cannot stone the King, striking the wood which bears his likeness.

Commentary.—Thus, every man who honours the image must necessarily honour the original.

The same.

Just as the man who shows contempt for the royal image is held to show it for the King himself, so is he convicted of sin who shows contempt for man made after an image.

St Athanasius, from the Hundred Chapters addressed to Antiochus, the Prefect, according to Question and Answer.— Chap. xxxviii.

Answer.—We, who are of the faithful, do not worship images as gods, as the heathens did, God forbid, but we mark our loving desire alone to see the face of the person represented in image. Hence, when it is obliterated, we are wont to throw the image as so much wood into the fire. Jacob, when he was about to die, worshipped on the point of Joseph's staff, not honouring the staff but its owner. Just in the same way do we greet images as we should embrace our children and parents to signify our affection. Thus the Jew, too, worshipped the tablets of the law, and the two golden cherubim in carved work, not because he honoured gold or stone for itself, but the Lord who had ordered them to be made.

St John Chrysostom, on the ' Third Psalm, on David, and Absalom.'

Kings put victorious trophies before their conquering generals; rulers erect proud monuments to their charioteers, and brave men, and with the epitaph as a crown, use matter for their triumph. Others, again, write the praises of conquerors in books, wishing to show that their own gift in praising is greater than those praised. And orators and painters, sculpturers and people, rulers, and cities, and places acclaim the victorious. No one ever made images of the deserter or the coward.

St Cyril of Alexandria, from his ' Address to the Emperor Theodosius.'

If images represent the originals, they should call forth the same reverence.

The same, from his ' Treasures.'

Images are ever the likenesses of their originals.

The same, from his Poem, on the 'Revelation of Christ being signified through all the Teaching of Moses. On Abraham and Melchisedech.'—Chap. vi.

Images should be made after their originals.

St Gregory of Nazianzen, from His Sermon on the 'Son,' ii.

An image is essentially a representation of its original.

St Chrysostom, from his Third 'Commentary on the Colossians.'

The image of what is invisible, were it also invisible, would cease to be an image. An image, as far as it is an image, should be kept inviolably by us, owing to the likeness it represents.

The same, from his 'Commentary on the Hebrews.'—Chap. xvii.

As in images the image presents the form of a man, though not his strength, so the original and the likeness have much in common, for the likeness is the man.

Eusebius Pamphilius, from the Fifth Book of his Gospel Proofs, on ' God appeared to Abraham by the Oak of Mambre.'

Hence, even now the inhabitants cherish the place where visions appeared to Abraham, as divinely consecrated. The turpentine tree is still to be seen, and those who received Abraham's hospitality are painted in picture, one on each side, and the stranger of greatest dignity in the middle. He would be an image of our Lord and Saviour, whom even rude men reverence, Whose divine words they believe. It was He who, through Abraham, sowed the seeds of piety in men. In the likeness and habit of an ordinary man He presented himself to Abraham,* and gave him knowledge of His Father.

John of Antioch, also called Malala, from his Chronography concerning the ' Woman with the Issue of Blood, who erected a Monument to Christ.'

From that time John the Baptist became known to men, and Herod, toparcha of the

---

* θεωφίλει προπάτορι.

Trachonitis region beheaded him in the city of Sebaste, on the eighth day of the kalends of June, Flaccus and Ruffinus being consuls. King Herod, Philip's son, in grief at this event, left Judea. A rich woman, Berenice by name, who was also living at Paneada, sought him out wishing as she had been cured by Jesus, to erect a monument to Him. Not daring to do it without the king's consent, she presented a petition to King Herod, asking to be allowed to erect a golden monument in that city to our Lord. The petition ran thus :—

To the august Herod, toparcha, law-giver of Jews and Greeks, King of Trachonitis, a suppliant petition from Berenice, an inhabitant of Paneada. You are crowned with justice and mercy and all other virtues. Knowing this and in good hope of success, I am writing to you. If you read my beginning you will soon be instructed as to facts. From childhood I suffered with an issue of blood, and spent my time and my substance on doctors, and was not cured. Hearing of the wonder-working Christ, how He raised the dead to life again, put forth devils, and cured the sick by one word, I also went to Him as to

God. And approaching the crowd which surrounded Him fearing lest He should turn me away in anger on account of my complaint, and that I should feel it more, I said to myself, 'If I could only touch the border of His garment, I should be cured.' I had no sooner touched it than the hæmorrhage stopped, and I was cured on the spot. And He, as if He had read my heart's desire, said aloud, 'Who has touched Me? Power has gone out of Me!' And I pale and trembling, thinking to throw off my sickness the sooner, prostrated myself at His feet, bathing the ground with my tears, and confessed my action. He in His goodness compassionating me, assured me of my cure, saying : 'Be of good heart, daughter, thy faith has healed thee. Go in peace!' Do you now, august ruler, grant my righteous petition. King Herod receiving this petition, was struck with wonder and in awe at the cure, replied : 'The cure wrought for you, O woman, deserves a splendid monument. Go then and put up any memorial you like to Him, in praise of the Healer.' And immediately Berenice the sick woman of yore, set up in the midst of her own city of Paneada a monument in bronze, adorned with gold and silver. It is still standing in the city of Paneada. Not long ago it was taken from the place where it stood to the middle of the city, and placed in a house of prayer. One, Batho, a converted Jew, found it mentioned in a book which contained an account of all those who had reigned over Judea.

From the 'Ecclesiastical History of Socrates,' Book I. Chap. xviii., on the Emperor Constantine.

After this the Emperor Constantine, being most zealous for the Christian religion, destroyed heathen observances, and prohibited single combats, whilst he set up his images in the temples.

Stephen Bostrenus, against the Jews.— Chap. iv.

We have made the images of the saints for a remembrance of Abraham, Isaac, Jacob, Moses, and Elias and Zachary, and of other prophets and holy martyrs, who gave their life for Him. Every one who looks at their images may thus be reminded of them and glorify Him who glorifies them.

The same.

As to images let us take courage that every work done in God's name is good and holy. Now as to idols and statues, beware, they are all bad, both the things and their makers. An image of a holy prophet is one thing, a statue or carved figure of Saturn or Venus, the sun or the moon, quite another. As man was made after God's image, he is worshipped; but the serpent as the image of the devil, is unclean and execrable. Tell me, O Jew, if you reject man's handiwork, what is left on earth to be worshipped which is not the work of his hand? Was not the ark made by hands, and the altar, the propitiatory and the cherubim, the golden urn containing the manna, the table and the inner tabernacle, and all that God ordered to be put in the holy of Holies? Were not the cherubim the images of angels made by hands? Do you call them idols? What do you say to Moses who worshipped them and to Israel? Worship is symbolical of honour, and we sinners worship God, and glorify Him by the divine worship of latreia which is due to Him, and we tremble before Him as our

Creator. We worship the angels and servants of God for His sake, as creatures and servants of God. An image is a name and likeness of him it represents. Thus both by writing and by engraving we are ever mindful of our Lord's sufferings, and of the holy prophets in the old law and in the new.

St Leontius of Naples, in Cyprus, against the Jews—Book v.

Enter then heartily into our apology for the making of sacred images, so that the mouths of foolish people speaking injustice may be closed. This tradition comes from the old law, not from us. Listen to God's command to Moses that he should make two cherubim wrought in metal to overshadow the propitiatory. And again, God showed the temple to Ezechiel, with its carved faces of lions, forms of palms and men from floor to ceiling. The command is truly awe-inspiring. God, who enjoins Israel not to make any graven thing, likeness or image of anything in heaven or on earth, also orders Moses to make carved cherubim. God shows the temple to

Ezechiel, full of images and sculptured likenesses of lions, palms, and men. And Solomon, in conformity to the law, filled the temple with metal figures of oxen, palms, and men, and God did not reproach him for it. Now, if you wish to reproach *me* concerning images, you condemn God, who ordered these things to be made that they might remind us of Himself.

The same, from the 3rd Book.

Again, atheists mock at us concerning the Holy Cross and the worship of divine images, calling us idolators and worshippers of wooden gods. Now, if I am a worshipper of wood, as you say, I am a worshipper of many, and, if so, I should swear by many, and say, ' By the gods,' just as you at the sight of one calf said, 'These are thy gods, O Israel.' You could not maintain that Christian lips had used the expression, but the adulterous and unbelieving synagogue is wont ever to cast infamy upon the all-wise Church of Christ.

The same.

We do not adore as gods the figures and

images of the saints. For if it was the mere wood of the image that we adored as God, we should likewise adore all wood, and not, as often happens, when the form grows faint, throw the image into the fire. And again, as long as the wood remains in the form of a cross, I adore it on account of Christ who was crucified upon it. When it falls to pieces, I throw them into the fire. Just as the man who receives the sealed orders of the king and embraces the seal, looks upon the dust and paper and wax as honourable in their reference to the king's service, so we Christians, in worshipping the Cross, do not worship the wood for itself, but seeing in it the impress and seal and figure of Christ Himself, crucified through it and on it, we fall down and adore.

The same.

On this account I depict Christ and His sufferings in churches, and houses, and public places, and images, on clothes, and store-houses, and in every available place, so that ever before me, I may bear them in lasting memory, and not be unmindful, as you are, of my Lord God. In worshipping the book of the law, you are not worshipping parchment or colour, but God's words contained in it. So do I worship the image of Christ, neither wood nor colouring for themselves. Adoring an inanimate figure of Christ through the Cross, I seem to possess and to adore Christ. Jacob received Joseph's cloak of many colours from his brothers who had sold him, and he caressed it with tears as he gazed at it. He did not weep over the cloak, but considered it a way of showing his love for Joseph and of embracing him. Thus do we Christians embrace with our lips the image of Christ, or the apostles, or the martyrs, whilst in spirit we deem that we are embracing Christ Himself or His martyr. As I have often said, the end in view must always be considered in all greeting and worship. If you upbraid me because I worship the wood of the Cross, why do you not upbraid Jacob for worshipping on the point of Joseph's staff? (ἐπὶ τὸ ἄκρον τῆς ῥάβδου). It is evident that it was not the wood he honoured by his worship, but Joseph, as we adore Christ through the Cross. Abraham worshipped impious men who sold him the cave, and bent his knee to the ground, yet he did not worship them as gods. And again, Jacob magnified impious Pharao and idolatrous Esau seven times, yet not as God. How many salutations and worshippings I have put before you, both natural and scriptural, which are not to be condemned, and you no sooner see any one worshipping the image of Christ or His Immaculate (παναγίας) Mother or a saint than you are angry and blaspheme and call me an idolator. Have you no shame, seeing me as you do day by day pulling down the temples of idols in the whole world and raising churches to martyrs? If I worship idols, why do I honour martyrs, their destroyers? If I glorify wood, as you say, why do I honour the saints who have pulled down the wooden statues of demons? If I glorify stones, how can I glorify the apostles who broke the stone idols? If I honour the images of false gods, how can I praise and glorify and keep the feast of the three children at Babylon who would not worship the golden statue? How greatly foolish people err, and how blind they are! What shamelessness is yours, O Jew! what impiety! You sin indeed against the truth. Arise, O God, and justify Thy cause. Judge and justify us from people, not all people, but from senseless and hostile people who constantly provoke Thee.

The same.

If, as I have often said, I worshipped wood and stone as God, I, too, should say to each, 'Thou hast brought me forth.' If I worship the images of the saints, or rather the saints, and worship and reverence the combats of the holy martyrs, how can you call these idols, senseless man? For idols are likenesses of false gods and adulterers, murderers and luxurious men, not of prophets or apostles. Listen whilst I take a telling and most true example of Christian and heathen images. The Chaldeans in Babylon had all sorts of musical instruments for the worship of idols who were devils, and the children of Israel had brought musical instruments from Jerusalem, which they hung upon the willow trees, and the instruments of both lutes and stringed instruments and flutes gave forth their music, these for the glory of God, the others for the service of devils. So must you look upon images and idols of heathens and Christians. Heathen idols were for the glory and remembrance of the devil; Christian images are for the glory of Christ, and of His apostles and martyrs and saints.

The same.

When, then, you see a Christian worshipping the Cross, know that his adoration is not given to the wood, but to Christ Crucified. We might as well worship all wood, as Israel worshipped woods and trees, saying, 'Thou art my God, and Thou hast brought me forth.' It is not so with us. We keep in churches and in our houses a remembrance and a representation of our Lord's sufferings and of those who fought for Him, doing everything for our Lord's sake.

Once more. Tell me, O Jew, what law authorised Moses to worship Jethor, his brother-in-law, and an idolator? Or Jacob to worship Pharao, and Abraham the sons of Emmor? They were just men and prophets. Again, Daniel worshipped the impious Nabuchodonosor. For if they so acted on account of life in this world, why do you reproach me for worshipping the holy memories of the saints, whether in books or pictures, their combats and sufferings, which are a daily source of good to me, and will help me to lasting and eternal life?

*Saint Athanasius against the Arians.—
Book iii.*

The Son being of the same substance as the Father, He can justly say that He has what the Father has. Hence it was fitting and proper that after the words 'I and the Father are one,' he should add, 'that you may know that I am in the Father and the Father in Me.' He had already said the same thing. 'He who sees Me sees the Father.' There is one and the same mind in these three sayings. To know that the Father and the Son are one is to know that he is in the Father and the Father in the Son. The Godhead of the Son is the Godhead of the Father. The man who receives this understands 'that he who sees the Son sees the Father.' For the Godhead of the Father is seen in the Son. This will be easier to understand from the example of the king's image which shows forth his form and likeness. The king is the likeness of his image. The likeness of the king is indelibly impressed upon the image, so that any one looking at the image sees the king, and again, any one looking at the king recognises that the image is his likeness. Being an indelible likeness, the image might answer a man, who expressed the wish to see the king after contemplating it, by saying, 'The king and I are one. I am in him and he is in me. That which you see in me you see in him, and the man who looks upon him looks at the same in me.' He who worships the image worships the king in it. The image is his form and likeness.

The same, to Antiochus the Ruler.

What do our adversaries say to these things, they who maintain that we should not worship the effigies of the saints, which are preserved amongst us for a remembrance of them.

St Ambrose of Milan, to the Emperor Gratian concerning the Incarnation of God the Word.

God before flesh was made, and God in the

flesh. There is a fear lest, abstracting the double principle of action and wisdom from Christ, we should glorify a mutilated Christ. Now, is it possible to divide Christ whilst we adore His Godhead and His flesh? Do we divide Him when we adore at once the image of God and the Cross? God forbid.

St Cyril of Jerusalem, twelfth Instruction.

If you seek the cause of Christ's presence, go back to the first chapter of Scripture. God made the world in six days, but the world was made for man. The most brilliant sun glowing with light was made for man. And all living things were created for our service, trees and flowers for our enjoyment. All created things were beautiful, yet only man was the image of God. The sun arose by command alone: man was moulded by the Divine Hand. 'Let us make man to our image and likeness.' The wooden image of an earthly king is honoured, how much more the rational image of God?

St John Chrysostom, on the Machabees.

The royal effigies are shown forth not only on

gold and silver, and the most costly materials, but the royal form itself, even on copper. The difference of matter does not affect the dignity of the character impressed, nor does a viler material diminish the honour of what is great. The royal figure is always a consecration; not lessened by matter, it exalts matter.

The same, against Julian the Apostate.—1st Book.

What does this new Nabuchodonosor want? He has not shown himself kinder to us than Nabuchodonosor of old, whose furnace still pierces us through, although we have escaped from its flames. Do not the shrines of saints in churches, inviting the worship of the faithful, show forth the destruction of the body?*

The same, on the Piscina.

Just as when the royal effigy and image is sent or carried into the city, rulers and people go out to meet it with respect and reverence, not honouring the wooden receptacle, or the waxen representation, but the person of the king; so is it with created things.

---

* οὐχὶ καὶ τα ἀναθήματα τῶν ἁγίων ἐπ' ἐκκλησίαις κείμενα εἰς προσκύνησιν τῶν πιστῶν, δηλοῦσι τὴν λώβην του σώματος.

Severianus of the Gabali, on the Cross.

Fourth Homily.—' Moses struck the rock twice.' Why twice? If he was obeying God's commands, what need was there of striking a second time? If without, not two, or ten, or a hundred strikings would have unlocked nature: if it was simply God's work without the mystery of the Cross, one striking, or nod, or word would have sufficed. But it is meant to be an image of the Cross. Moses, the Scripture says, struck once and then again, in the sign of the Cross, not for actual necessity, so that inanimate nature might reverence the symbol. If in the king's absence his image supplies his place, rulers worship, and festivals are held, and princes go out to meet it, and people prostrate themselves, not looking at the material, but at the figure of the king shown forth in representation not seen in nature, how much more shall the image of the Eternal King break open the heavens and the whole universe, not the rock alone.

Jerome, Priest of Jerusalem, on the Holy Trinity.

As the Scripture nowhere enjoins you to worship the Cross, what makes you adore it? Tell us, Jews and heathens, and all inquiring people.

Answer.—On this account, O slow and foolish of heart, God allowed the people, who revered Him, to worship what was on earth, the handiwork of man, so that they should not be able to reproach Christians concerning the Cross and the worship of images. Now just as the Jew adored the ark of the covenant, and the two carved cherubim of gold, and the two tablets of Moses, although there is nowhere an order from God to worship or revere them, so is it with Christians. We do not revere the Cross as God; we show through it what we truly feel about the Crucified One.

Simeon of Mount Thaumastus on Images.

Possibly a contentious unbeliever will maintain that we worshipping images in our churches are convicted of praying to lifeless idols. Far be it from us to do this. Faith* makes Christians, and God, who cannot deceive, works miracles. We do not rest contented with mere colouring. With the material picture before our eyes we see the invisible God through the visible representation, and glorify Him as if present, not as a God without reality, but as God who is the essence of being. Nor are the saints whom we glorify fictitious. They are in being, and are living with God; and their spirits being holy, they help, by the power of God, those who deserve and need their assistance.

Athanasius, Archbishop of Antioch, to Simeon, Bishop of the Bostri, on the Sabbath.

Just as in the king's absence his image is worshipped, so in his presence it is extravagant to leave the original to pay homage to the image. It is disregarded, because the original on whose account it is honoured is present, but that is no reason for dishonouring it. It is much the same, I think, with the shadow or letter of the law. The apostle

---

* τα γὰρ τῶν χριστιανῶν πιστίς ἐστί, καὶ ὁ ἀψευδὴς ἡμῶν θεὸς ἐνεργεῖ τας δυνάμεις.

calls it a figure. In so far as grace anticipated the reign of truth, the saints were types, contemplating the truth as in a glass. When the promises were fulfilled, it was no longer desirable to live according to types, nor to follow them. In the presence of the realisation the type vanishes into insignificance. Still they did not dishonour nor deride types; they honoured them, and judged those who treated them with contumely impious, and deserving of death and severe chastisement.

The same.—3rd Homily.

A man worships the king's image for the honour due to the king, the image itself being mere wax and paint.

St Athanasius of Mount Sinai on the New Sabbath, and on St Thomas the Apostle.

Those who saw Christ in the flesh looked upon Him as a prophet. We, who have not seen Him, have confessed Him from our childhood to be the great and Almighty God Himself, the Creator of eternity, and splendour of the Father. We listen with faith to His Gospel, as if we saw Christ Himself speaking.

And receiving the pure treasure of His body, we believe that Christ Himself is acting in us. And if we see only the image of His divine form, as if looking down upon us from heaven, we prostrate and adore. Great is now the faith of Christ.

From the Life of the Abbot Daniel, on Eulogius the Quarryman.

Then he went away dejected, and threw himself before an image of Our Lady, and crying out, he said: 'Lord, enable me to pay what I promised this man.'

From the Life of St Mary of Egypt.

As I was weeping, I lifted up my eyes and saw the image of Our Lady, and I said to her:—

'O Virgin, Mother of God (θεότοκε δέσποινα), who didst give birth to God the Word, I know that it is neither fitting nor seemly that one so defiled and so covered with guilt as I should look up to thy image, O ever Virgin. It is fitting that I should be hated and shunned by thy purity. Yet as He who was born of thee became man on purpose to call sinners to repentance, help me, for I have no other succour. Let me also find an entrance. Do not refuse me a sight of the wood on which God the Word, thy Son, suffered according to the flesh, who shed His own precious blood for me. Grant, O Queen, that I may be admitted to worship the sacred Cross, and I will promise thee as surety to the God whom thou didst bring forth that I will keep myself ever undefiled. When I see the Cross of thy Son, I will at once renounce the world and the things of the world, and forthwith follow wherever thou shalt lead.'

Saying this, taking faith's token as a conviction, encouraged by Our Lady's clemency, I left that place where I had made my petition, and returned again to join those who were entering the edifice. No one thrust me aside, and no one prevented me from going into the church. Then I was seized with horror and fear and trembling in all my limbs. Throwing myself on the ground, and worshipping that holy floor, I came out, and went to her who had promised to be my security. When I came to the place in which the agreement had been signed, I knelt down before the ever blessed Virgin, Mother of God, and addressed her in these words :—

'O loving Queen (φιλάγαθε δέσποινα), thou hast shown me thy goodness; thou didst not despise the petition of my unworthiness. I have seen glory which sinners do not see. Praise be to God who receives the repentance of sinners through thee.'

St Methodius, Bishop of the Patari (παταρών), on the Resurrection.

The images of earthly kings, even if they are not made of finest gold and silver, command at once honour from all. As men are not honouring matter, they do not choose the most precious from the less precious; they honour the image, whether made of putty or of copper. A derider of either, whether he shows contempt to the image of plaster or of gold, will be held to show contempt to his lord and king. We make golden images of His angels, principalities, or powers, for His honour and glory.

SERMON I

ON THE ASSUMPTION (κοίμησις).

THE memory of the just takes place with rejoicing, said Solomon, the wisest of men; for precious in God's sight is the death of His saints, according to the royal * David. If, then, the memory of all the just is a subject of rejoicing, who will not offer praise to justice in its source, and holiness in its treasure-house? It is not mere praise; it is praising with the intention of gaining eternal glory. God's dwelling-place does not need our praise, that city of God, concerning which great things were spoken, as holy. † David addresses it in these words: 'Glorious things are said of thee, thou city of God.' What sort of city shall we choose for the invisible and uncircumscribed God, who holds all things in His hand, if not

---

* θεοπάτωρ.   † θεῖος.

that city which alone is above nature, giving shelter without circumscription* to the supersubstantial Word of God? Glorious things have been spoken of that city by God himself. For what is more exalted than being made the recipient of God's counsel, which is from all eternity?

Neither human tongue nor angelic mind is able worthily to praise her through whom it is given to us to look clearly upon the Lord's glory. What then? Shall we be silent through fear of our insufficiency? Certainly not. Shall we be trespassers beyond our own boundaries, and freely handle ineffable mysteries, putting off all restraint? By no means. Mingling, rather, fear with desire, and weaving them into one crown, with reverent hand and longing soul, let us show forth the poor first-fruits of our intelligence, in gratitude to our Queen and Mother, the benefactress of all creation, as a repayment of our debt. A story is told of some rustics who were ploughing up the soil when a king chanced to pass, in the splendour of his royal robes and crown, and surrounded by countless gift bearers, standing in a circle.

* ἀπεριγράπτως.

As there was no gift to offer at that moment, one of them was collecting water in his hands, as there happened to be a copious stream near by. Of this he prepared a gift for the king, who addressed him in these words: 'What is this, my boy?' And he answered boldly: 'I made the best of what I had, thinking it was better to show my willingness, than to offer nothing. You do not need our gifts, nor do you wish for anything from us save our good will. The need is on our side, and the reward is in the doing. I know that glory often comes to the grateful.'

The king in wonder praised the boy's cleverness, graciously acknowledged his willingness, and made him many rich gifts in return. Now, if that proud monarch so generously rewarded good intentions, will not Our Lady ($\dot{\eta}$ ὄντως ἀγαθὴ δέσποινα), the Mother of God, accept *our* good will, not judging us by what we accomplish? Our Lady is the Mother of God, who alone is good and infinite in His condescension, who preferred the two mites to many splendid gifts. She will indeed receive us, who are paying off our debt, and make us a return out of all proportion to what we offer. Since prayer is absolutely necessary for our needs, let us direct our attention to it.

What shall we say, O Queen? What words shall we use? What praise shall we pour upon thy sacred and glorified head, thou giver of good gifts and of riches, the pride of the human race, the glory of all creation, through whom it is truly blessed. He whom nature did not contain in the beginning, was born of thee. The Invisible One is contemplated face to face. O Word of God, do Thou open my slow lips, and give their utterances Thy richest blessing; inflame us with the grace of Thy Spirit, through whom fishermen became orators, and ignorant men spoke supernatural wisdom, so that our feeble voices may contribute to thy loved Mother's praises, even though greatness should be extolled by misery. She, the chosen one of an ancient race, by a predetermined counsel and the good pleasure of God the Father, who had begotten Thee in eternity immaterially, brought Thee forth in the latter times, Thou who art propitiation and salvation, justice and redemption, life of life, light of light, and true God of true God.

The birth of her, whose Child was marvellous, was above nature and understanding, and it was salvation to the world ; her death was glorious, and truly a sacred feast. The Father predestined her, the prophets foretold her through the Holy Ghost. His sanctifying power overshadowed her, cleansed* and made her holy, and, as it were, predestined her. Then Thou, Word of the Father, not dwelling in place,† didst invite the lowliness of our nature to be united to the immeasurable greatness of Thy inscrutable Godhead. Thou, who didst take flesh of the Blessed Virgin, vivified by a reasoning soul, having first abided in her undefiled and immaculate womb, creating Thyself, and causing her to exist in Thee, didst become perfect man,, not ceasing to be perfect God, equal to Thy Father, but taking upon Thyself our weakness through ineffable goodness. Through it Thou art one Christ, one Lord, one Son of God, and man at the same time, perfect God and perfect man, wholly God and wholly man, one substance (ὑπόστασις) from two perfect natures, the Godhead and the manhood. And in two perfect natures, the divine and the human, God is not pure God,

---

* ἐκάθηρε τε καὶ ἡγίασε.   † ἀπεριγράπτως κατῴκησας.

nor the man only man, but the Son of God and the Incarnate God are one and the same God and man without confusion or division, uniting in Himself substantially the attributes of both natures. Thus, He is at once uncreated and created, mortal and immortal, visible and invisible, in place and not in place. He has a divine will and a human will, a divine action and a human also, two powers of choosing (αὐτεξούσια) divine and human. He shows forth divine wonders and human affections,—natural, I mean, and pure. Thou hast taken upon Thyself, Lord, of Thy great mercy, the state of Adam as he was before the fall, body, soul, and mind, and all that they involve physically, so as to give me a perfect salvation. It is true indeed that what was not assumed was not healed.* Having thus become the mediator between God and man, Thou didst destroy enmity, and lead back to Thy Father those who had deserted Him, wanderers to their home, and those in darkness to the light. Thou didst bring pardon to the contrite, and didst change mortality into immortality. Thou didst deliver the world from the aberration of

* ὄντως γὰρ τὸ ἀπρόσληπτον ἀθεράπευτον.

many gods, and didst make men the children of God, partakers of Thy divine glory. Thou didst raise the human race, which was condemned to hell, above all power and majesty, and in Thy person it is seated on the King's eternal throne. Who was the instrument of these infinite benefits exceeding all mind and comprehension, if not the Mother ever Virgin who bore Thee?

Realise, Beloved in the Lord, the grace of to-day, and its wondrous solemnity. Its mysteries are not terrible, nor do they inspire awe. Blessed are they who have eyes to see. Blessed are they who see with spiritual eyes. This night shines as the day. What countless angels acclaim the death of the life-giving Mother! How the eloquence of apostles blesses the departure of this body which was the receptacle of God. How the Word of God, who deigned in His mercy to become her Son, ministering with His divine hands to this immaculate and divine being,* as His mother, receives her holy soul. O wondrous Law-giver, fulfilling the law which He had Himself laid down, not being bound by it, for it was He who enjoined children to show reverence to

* . . . τῇ παναγίᾳ ταύτῃ καὶ θειοτάτῃ.

their parents. 'Honour thy father and thy mother,' He says. The truth of this is apparent to every one, calling to mind even dimly the words of holy Scripture. If according to it the souls of the just are in the hands of God, how much more is her soul in the hands of her Son and her God. This is indisputable. Let us consider who she is and whence she came, how she, the greatest and dearest of all God's gifts, was given to this world. Let us examine what her life was, and the mysteries in which she took part. Heathens in the use of funeral orations most carefully brought forward anything which could be turned to praise of the deceased, and at the same time encourage the living to virtue, drawing generally upon fable and fiction, not having fact to go upon. How then, shall we not deserve scorn if we bury in silence that which is most true and sacred, and in very deed the source of praise and salvation to all? Shall we not receive the same punishment as the man who hid his master's talent? Let us adapt our subject to the needs of those who listen, as food is suited to the body.

Joachim and Anne were the parents of Mary. Joachim kept as strict a watch over his thoughts as a shepherd over his flock, having them entirely under his control. For the Lord God led him as a sheep, and he wanted for none of the best things. When I say best, let no one think I mean what is commonly acceptable to the multitude, that upon which greedy minds are fixed, the pleasures of life that can neither endure nor make their possessors better, nor confer real strength. They follow the downward course of human life and cease all in a moment, even if they abounded before. Far be it from us to cherish these things, nor is this the portion of those who fear God. But the good things which are a matter of desire to those who possess true knowledge, delighting God, and fruitful to their possessors, namely, virtues, bearing fruit in due season, that is, in eternity, will reward with eternal life those who have laboured worthily and have persevered in their acquisition as far as possible. The labour goes before, eternal happiness follows. Joachim ever shepherded his thoughts. In the place of pastures, dwelling by contemplation on the words of sacred Scripture, made glad on the restful waters of divine grace, withdrawn from foolishness, he walked in the path of justice. And Anne, whose name means grace, was no less a companion in her life than a wife, blessed with all good gifts, though afflicted for a mystical reason with sterility. Grace in very truth remained sterile, not being able to produce fruit in the souls of men. Therefore, men declined from good and degenerated; there was not one of understanding nor one who sought after God. Then His divine goodness, taking pity on the work of His hands, and wishing to save it, put an end to that mystical barrenness, that of holy (θεόφρονος) Anne, I mean, and she gave birth to a child, whose equal had never been created and never can be. The end of barrenness proved clearly that the world's sterility would cease and that the withered trunk would be crowned with vigorous and mystical life.

Hence the Mother of our Lord is announced. An angel foretells her birth. It was fitting that in this, too, she, who was to be the human Mother of the one true and living God, should be marked out above every one else. Then she was offered in God's holy temple, and remained there, showing to all a great example of zeal and holiness, withdrawn from frivolous society. When, however, she reached full age and the law required that she should leave the temple, she was entrusted by the priests to Joseph, her bridegroom, as the guardian of her virginity, a steadfast observer of the law from his youth. Mary, the holy and undefiled (πανάμωμος), went to Joseph, contenting herself with her household matters, and knowing nothing beyond her four walls.

In the fulness of time, as the divine apostle says, the angel Gabriel was sent to this true child of God, and saluted her in the words, 'Hail, full of grace, the Lord is with thee.' Beautiful is the angel's salutation to her who is greater than an angel. He is the bearer of joy to the whole world. She was troubled at his words, not being used to speak with men, for she had resolved to keep her virginity unsullied. She pondered in herself what this greeting might be. Then the angel said to her: 'Fear not, Mary. Thou hast found grace before God.' In very deed, she who was worthy of grace had found it. She found grace who had done the deeds of grace, and had reaped its fulness. She found grace who brought forth the source of grace, and was a rich harvest of grace. She found an abyss of grace who kept undefiled her double virginity, her virginal soul no less spotless than her body; hence her perfect virginity. 'Thou shalt bring forth a Son,' he said, 'and shalt call His name Jesus' (Jesus is interpreted Saviour). 'He shall save His people from their sins.' What did she, who is true wisdom, reply? She does not imitate our first mother Eve, but rather improves upon her incautiousness, and calling in nature to support her, thus answers the angel: 'How is this to be, since I know not man? What you say is impossible, for it goes beyond the natural laws laid down by the Creator. I will not be called a second Eve and disobey the will of my God. If you are not speaking godless things, explain the mystery by saying how it is to be accomplished.' Then the messenger of truth answered her: 'The Holy Spirit shall come to thee, and the power of the Most High shall overshadow thee. Therefore He who is born to thee shall be called the Son of God.' That which is foretold is not subservient to the laws of nature. For God, the Creator of nature, can alter its laws. And she, listening in holy reverence to that sacred name, which she had ever desired, signified her obedience in words full of humility and joy: 'Behold the handmaid of the Lord. Be it done unto me according to thy word.'

'O the depth of the riches, of the wisdom, and of the knowledge of God,' I will exclaim in the apostle's words. 'How incomprehensible are His judgments, and how unsearchable His ways.' O inexhaustible goodness of God! O boundless goodness! He who called what was not into being, and filled heaven and earth, whose throne is heaven, and whose footstool is the earth, a spacious dwelling-place, made the womb of His own servant, and in it the mystery of mysteries is accomplished (τὸ πάντων καινῶν καινότερον ἀποτελεῖ μυστήριον). Being God He becomes man, and is marvellously brought forth without detriment to the virginity of His Mother. And He is lifted up as a baby in earthly arms, who is the brightness of eternal glory, the form of the Father's substance, by the word of whose mouth all created things exist. O truly divine wonder! O mystery transcending all nature and understanding! O marvellous virginity! What, O holy Mother and Virgin, is this great mystery accomplished in thee? Blessed art thou amongst women, and blessed is the fruit of thy womb. Thou art blessed from generation to generation, thou who alone art worthy of being blessed. Behold all generations shall call thee blessed as thou hast said. The daughters of Jerusalem, I mean, of the Church, saw thee. Queens have blessed thee, that is, the spirits of the just, and they shall praise thee for ever. Thou art the royal throne which angels surround, seeing upon it their very King and Lord. Thou art a spiritual Eden, holier and diviner than Eden of old. That Eden was the abode of the mortal Adam, whilst the Lord came from heaven to dwell in thee. The ark foreshadowed thee who hast kept the seed of the new world. Thou didst bring forth Christ, the salvation of the world, who destroyed sin and its angry waves. The burning bush was a figure of thee, and the tablets of the law, and the ark of the testament. The golden urn and candelabra, the table and the flowering rod of Aaron were significant types of thee. From thee arose the splendour of the Godhead, the eternal Word of the Father, the most sweet and heavenly Manna, the sacred Name above every name, the Light which was from the beginning. The heavenly Bread of Life, the Fruit without seed, took flesh of thee. Did not that flame foreshadow thee with its burning fire an image of the divine fire within thee? And Abraham's tent most clearly pointed to thee. By the Word of God dwelling in thee human nature produced the bread made of ashes, its first fruits, from thy most pure womb, the first fruits kneaded into bread and cooked by divine fire, becoming His divine person, and His true substance of a living body quickened by a reasoning and intelligent soul.* I had nearly forgotten Jacob's ladder. Is it not evident to every one that it prefigured thee, and is not the type easily recognised? Just as Jacob saw the ladder bringing together heaven and earth, and on it angels coming down and going up, and the truly strong and invulnerable God

* τῷ γὰρ θεῷ λόγῳ ἐν τῇ γαστρί σου σκηνώσαντι ἀνθρωπεία φύσις τὸν ἐγκρυφίαν ἄρτον, τὴν ἑαυτῆς ἀπαρχὴν ἐκ τῶν σῶν ἁγνῶν αἱμάτων προσήγαγεν, ὀπτωμένην πῶς καὶ ἀρτοποιουμένην ὑπὸ τοῦ θείου πυρός, etc.

wrestling mystically with himself, so art thou placed between us, and art become the ladder of God's intercourse with us, of Him who took upon Himself our weakness, uniting us to Himself, and enabling man to see God. Thou hast brought together what was parted. Hence angels descended to Him, ministering to Him as their God and Lord, and men, adopting the life of angels, are carried up to heaven.

How shall I understand the prediction of prophets? Shall I not refer them to thee, as we can prove them to be true? What is the fleece of David which receives the Son of the Almighty God, co-eternal and co-equal with His Father, as rain falls upon the soil? Does it not signify thee in thy bright shining? Who is the virgin foretold by Isaias who should conceive and bear a Son, God ever present with us, that is, who being born a man should remain God? What is Daniel's mountain from which arose Christ, the Corner-Stone, not made by the hand of man? Is it not thee, conceiving without man and still remaining a virgin? Let the inspired Ezechiel come forth and show us the closed gate, sealed by the Lord, and not yielding, according to his prophecy—let him point to its fulfilment in thee. The Lord of all came to thee, and taking flesh did not open the door of thy virginity. The seal remains intact. The prophets, then, foretell thee. Angels and apostles minister to thee, O Mother of God, ever Virgin, and John the virgin apostle. Angels and the spirits of the just, patriarchs and prophets surround thee to-day in thy departure to thy Son. Apostles watched over the countless host of the just who were gathered together from every corner of the earth by the divine commands, as a cloud around the divine and living Jerusalem, singing hymns of praise to thee, the author of our Lord's life-giving body.

O how does the source of life pass through death to life? O how can she obey the law of nature, who, in conceiving, surpasses the boundaries of nature? How is her spotless body made subject to death? In order to be clothed with immortality she must first put off mortality, since the Lord of nature did not reject the penalty of death. She dies according to the flesh, destroys death by death, and through corruption gains incorruption ($\phi\theta o\rho\hat{q}$

τὴν ἀφθαρσιαν χαρίζεται), and makes her death the source of resurrection. O how does Almighty God receive with His own hands the holy disembodied soul of our Lord's Mother! He honours her truly, whom being His servant by nature, He made His Mother, in His inscrutable abyss of mercy, when He became incarnate in very truth. We may well believe that the angelic choirs waited to receive thy departing soul. O what a blessed departure this going to God of thine. If God vouchsafes it to all His servants—and we know that He does—what an immense difference there is between His servants and His Mother. What, then, shall we call this mystery of thine? Death? Thy blessed soul is naturally parted from thy blissful and undefiled body, and the body is delivered to the grave, yet it does not endure in death, nor is it the prey of corruption. The body of her, whose virginity remained unspotted in child-birth, was preserved in its incorruption, and was taken to a better, diviner place, where death is not, but eternal life. Just as the glorious sun may be hidden momentarily by the opaque moon, it shows still though covered, and its rays illumine the darkness since light belongs to its essence. It has in itself a perpetual source of light, or rather it is the source of light as God created it. So art thou the perennial source of true light, the treasury of life itself, the richness of grace, the cause and medium of all our goods. And if for a time thou art hidden by the death of the body, without speaking, thou art our light, life-giving ambrosia, true happiness, a sea of grace, a fountain of healing and of perpetual blessing. Thou art as a fruitful tree in the forest, and thy fruit is sweet in the mouth of the faithful. Therefore I will not call thy sacred transformation death, but rest or going home, and it is more truly a going home. Putting off corporeal things, thou dwellest in a happier state.

Angels with archangels bear thee up. Impure spirits trembled at thy departure. The air raises a hymn of praise at thy passage, and the atmosphere is purified. Heaven receives thy soul with joy. The heavenly powers greet thee with sacred canticles and with joyous praise, saying: 'Who is this most pure creature ascending, shining as the dawn, beautiful as the moon, conspicuous as the sun? How sweet and lovely thou art, the lily of the field, the rose among thorns; therefore the young maidens loved thee. We are drawn after the odour of thy ointments. The King introduced thee into His chamber. There Powers protect thee, Principalities praise thee, Thrones proclaim thee, Cherubim are hushed in joy, and Seraphim magnify the true Mother by nature and by grace of their very Lord. Thou wert not taken into heaven as Elias was, nor didst thou penetrate to the third heaven with Paul, but thou didst reach the royal throne itself of thy Son, seeing it with thy own eyes, standing by it in joy and unspeakable familiarity. O gladness of angels and of all heavenly powers, sweetness of patriarchs and of the just, perpetual exultation of prophets, rejoicing the world and sanctifying all things, refreshment of the weary, comfort of the sorrowful, remission of sins, health of the sick, harbour of the storm-tossed, lasting strength of mourners, and perpetual succour of all who invoke thee.'

O wonder surpassing nature and creating wonder! Death, which of old was feared and hated, is a matter of praise and blessing. Of old it was the harbinger of grief, dejection, tears, and sadness, and now it is shown forth as the cause of joy and rejoicing. In the case of all God's servants, whose death is extolled, His good pleasure is surmised from their holy end, and therefore their death is blessed. It shows them to be perfect, blessed and immoveable in goodness, as the proverb says: 'Praise no man before his death.' This, however, we do not apply to thee. Thy blessedness was not death, nor was dying thy perfection, nor, again, did thy departure hence help thee to security. Thou art the beginning, middle, and end of all goods transcending mind, for thy Son in His conception and divine dwelling in thee is made our sure and true security. Thus thy words were true: from the moment of His conception, not from thy death, thou didst say all generations should call thee blessed. It was thou who didst break the force of death, paying its penalty, and making it gracious. Hence, when thy holy and sinless body was taken to the tomb, the choirs of angels bore it, and were all around, leaving nothing undone for the honour of our Lord's Mother, whilst apostles and all the assembly of the Church burst into prophetic song, saying: 'We shall be filled with the good things of Thy house, holy is Thy temple, wonderful in justice.' And again: 'The Most High has sanctified His tabernacle. The mountain of God is a fertile mountain, the mountain in which it pleased God to dwell.' The apostolic band lifting the true ark of the Lord God on their shoulders, as the priests of old the typical ark, and placing thy body in the tomb, made it, as if another Jordan, the way to the true land of the gospel, the heavenly Jerusalem, the mother of all the faithful, God being its Lord and architect. Thy soul did not descend to Limbo, neither did thy flesh see corruption. Thy pure and spotless body was not left in the earth, but the abode of the Queen, of God's true Mother, was fixed in the heavenly kingdom alone.

O how did heaven receive her who is greater than heaven? How did she, who had received God, descend into the grave? This truly happened, and she was held by the tomb. It was not after bodily wise that she surpassed heaven. For how can a body measuring three cubits, and continually losing flesh, be compared with the dimensions of heaven? It was rather by grace that she surpassed all height and depth, for that which is divine is incomparable. O sacred and wonderful, holy and worshipful body, ministered to now by angels, standing by in lowly reverence. Demons tremble: men approach with faith, honouring and worshipping her, greeting her with eyes and lips, and drawing down upon themselves abundant blessings. Just as a rich scent sprinkled upon clothes or places, leaves its fragrance even after it has been withdrawn, so now that holy, undefiled, and divine body, filled with heavenly fragrance, the rich source of grace, is laid in the tomb that it may be translated to a higher and better place. Nor did she leave the grave empty; her body imparted to it a divine fragrance, a source of healing, and of all good for those who approach it with faith.

We, too, approach thee to-day, O Queen; and again, I say, O Queen, O Virgin Mother of God, staying our souls with our trust in thee, as with a strong anchor. Lifting up mind, soul and body, and all ourselves to thee, rejoicing in psalms and hymns and spiritual canticles, we reach through thee One who is beyond our reach on account of His Majesty. If, as the divine Word made flesh taught us, honour shown to servants is honour shown to our common Lord, how can honour shown to thee, His Mother, be slighted? How is it not most desirable? Art thou not honoured as the very breath of life? Thus shall we best show our service to our Lord Himself. What do I say to our Lord? It is sufficient that those who think of Thee should recall the memory of Thy most precious gift as the cause of our lasting joy. How it fills us with gladness! How the mind that dwells on this holy treasury of Thy grace enriches itself.

This is our thank-offering to thee, the first fruits of our discourses, the best homage of my poor mind, whilst I am moved by desire of thee, and full of my own misery. But do thou graciously receive my desire, knowing that it exceeds my power. Watch over us, O Queen, the dwelling-place of our Lord. Lead and govern all our ways as thou wilt. Save us from our sins. Lead us into the calm harbour of the divine will. Make us worthy of future happiness through the sweet and face-to-face vision of the Word made flesh through thee. With Him, glory, praise, power, and majesty be to the Father and to the holy and life-giving Spirit, now and for ever. Amen.

SERMON II

ON THE ASSUMPTION (κοίμησις).

THERE is no one in existence who is able to praise worthily the holy death of God's Mother, even if he should have a thousand tongues and a thousand mouths. Not if all the most eloquent tongues could be united would their praises be sufficient. She is greater than all praise. Since, however, God is pleased with the efforts of a loving zeal, and the Mother of God with what concerns the service of her Son, suffer me now to revert again to her praises. This is in obedience to your orders, most excellent pastors, so dear to God, and we call upon the Word made flesh of her to come to our assistance. He gives speech to every mouth which is opened for Him. He is her sole pleasure and adornment. We know that in celebrating her praises we pay off our debt, and that in so doing we are again debtors, so that the debt is ever beginning afresh. It is fitting that we should exalt her who is above all created things, governing them as Mother of the God who is their Creator, Lord, and Master. Bear with me you who hang upon the divine words, and receive my good will. Strengthen my desire, and be patient with the weakness of my words. It is as if a man were to bring a violet of royal purple out of season, or a fragrant rose with buds of different hues, or some rich fruit of autumn to a mighty potentate who is divinely appointed to rule over men. Every day he sits at a table laden with every conceivable dish in the perfumed courts of his palace. He does not look at the smallness of the offering, or at its novelty so much as he admires the good intention, and with reason. This he would reward with an abundance of gifts and favours. So we, in our winter of poverty,* bring garlands to our Queen,

---

* οὕτω καὶ ἡμεῖς ἐν χειμῶνι τῶν ἐπῶν τὰ ἄνθη τῇ βασιλίδι προσάγοντες, καὶ γεγηρακότα λόγον πρὸς τοὺς ἀγῶνας τῶν ἐγκωμίων ὁπλίζοντες, καὶ τοῦ πόθου τῷ νῷ λίθον οἷα σιδήρῳ προστρίψαντες, ἢ ὡς βόρθρην δῶρον ἐκθλίψαντες, τὴν μυθοτόκον διάνοιαν, ἀμυδρόν τινα σπινθῆρα καὶ τρουγα λόγου τοῖς φιλολόγοις ὑμῖν καὶ φιλακροάμοσι νέμοντες, μᾶλλον καὶ μᾶλλον ἀποδειχθείημεν.

and prepare a flower of oratory for the feast of praise. We break our mind's stony desire with iron, pressing, as it were, the unripe grapes. And may you receive with more and more favour the words which fall upon your eager and listening ears.

What shall we offer the Mother of the Word if not our words? Like rejoices in like and in what it loves. Thus, then, making a start and loosening the reins of my discourse, I may send it forth as a charger ready equipped for the race. But do Thou, O Word of God, be my helper and auxiliary, and speak wisdom to my unwisdom. By Thy word make my path clear, and direct my course according to Thy good pleasure, which is the end of all wisdom and discernment.

To-day the holy Virgin of Virgins is presented in the heavenly temple. Virginity in her was so strong as to be a consuming fire. It is forfeited in every case by child-birth. But she is ever a virgin, before the event, in the birth itself, and afterwards. To-day the sacred and living ark of the living God, who conceived her Creator Himself, takes up her abode in the temple of God, not made by hands. David, her forefather,* rejoices. Angels and Archangels are in jubilation, Powers exult, Principalities and Dominations, Virtues and Thrones are in gladness: Cherubim and Seraphim magnify God. Not the least of their praise is it to refer praise to the Mother of glory. To-day the holy dove, the pure and guileless soul, sanctified by the Holy Spirit, putting off the ark of her body, the life-giving receptacle of Our Lord, found rest to the soles of her feet, taking her flight to the spiritual world, and dwelling securely in the sinless country above. To-day the Eden of the new Adam receives the true paradise, in which sin is remitted and the tree of life grows, and our nakedness is covered. For we are no longer naked and uncovered, and unable to bear the splendour of the divine likeness. Strengthened with the abundant grace of the Spirit, we shall no longer betray our nakedness in the words : 'I have put off my garment, how shall I put it on?' The serpent, by whose deceitful promise we were likened to brute beasts, did not enter into this paradise. He, the only begotten Son of God, God himself, of the same substance as the Father, took His

* θεοπάτωρ.

human nature of the pure Virgin. Being constituted a man, He made mortality immortal, and was clothed as a man. Putting aside corruption, He was indued with the incorruptibility of the Godhead.

To-day the spotless Virgin, untouched by earthly affections, and all heavenly in her thoughts, was not dissolved in earth, but truly entering heaven, dwells in the heavenly tabernacles. Who would be wrong to call her heaven, unless indeed he truly said that she is greater than heaven in surpassing dignity? The Lord and Creator of heaven, the Architect of all things beneath the earth and above, of creation, visible and invisible, Who is not circumvented by place (if that which surrounds things is rightly termed place), created Himself, without human co-operation, an Infant in her. He made her a rich treasure-house of His all-pervading and alone uncircumscribed Godhead, subsisting entirely in her without passion, remaining entire in His universality and Himself uncircumscribed. To-day the life-giving treasury and abyss of charity (I know not how to trust my lips to speak of it) is hidden in immortal death. She meets it without fear, who conceived death's destroyer, if indeed we may call her holy and vivifying departure by the name of death. For how could she, who brought life to all, be under the dominion of death? But she obeys the law of her own Son, and inherits this chastisement as a daughter of the first Adam, since her Son, who is the life, did not refuse it. As the Mother of the living God, she goes through death to Him. For if God said: 'Unless the first man put out his hand to take and taste of the tree of life, he shall live for ever,' how shall she, who received the Life Himself, without beginning or end, or finite vicissitudes, not live for ever.

Of old the Lord God banished from the garden of Eden our first parents after their disobedience, when they had dulled the eye of their heart through their sin, and weakened their mind's discernment, and had fallen into death-like apathy. But, now, shall not paradise receive her, who broke the bondage of all passion, sowed the seed of obedience to God and the Father, and was the beginning of life to the whole human race? Will not heaven open its gates to her with rejoicing? Yes, indeed. Eve listened to the serpent, adopted his suggestion, was caught by the lure of false and deceptive pleasure, and was condemned to pain and sorrow, and to bear children in suffering. With Adam she received the sentence of death, and was placed in the recesses of Limbo. How can death claim as its prey this truly blessed one, who listened to God's word in humility, and was filled with the Spirit, conceiving the Father's gift through the archangel, bearing without concupiscence or the co-operation of man the Person of the Divine Word, who fills all things, bringing Him forth without the pains of childbirth, being wholly united to God? How could Limbo open its gates to her? How could corruption touch the life-giving body? These are things quite foreign to the soul and body of God's Mother. Death trembled before her. In approaching her Son, death had learnt experience from His sufferings, and had grown wiser. The gloomy descent to hell was not for her, but a joyous, easy, and sweet passage to heaven. If, as Christ, the Life and the Truth says: 'Wherever I am, there is also my minister,' how much more shall not His mother be with Him? She brought Him forth without pain, and her death, also, was painless.

The death of sinners is terrible, for in it, sin, the cause of death, is sacrificed. What shall we say of her if not that she is the beginning of perpetual life. Precious indeed is the death of His saints to the Lord God of powers. More than precious is the passing away of God's Mother. Now let the heavens and the angels rejoice: let the earth and men be full of gladness. Let the air resound with song and canticle, and dark night put off its gloom, and emulate the brightness of day through the scintillating stars. The living city of the Lord God is assumed from God's temple, the visible Sion, and kings bring forth His most precious gift, their mother, to the heavenly Jerusalem,—that is to say, the apostles constituted princes by Christ, over all the earth, accompany the ever virginal Mother of God.

It seems to me not superfluous to bring forward and insist on the past types of this holy one, the Mother of God. These types succinctly announced the Divine Child whom we have received. I look upon His Mother as the saint of saints, the holiest of all, the fragrant urn for the manna, or rather, to speak more truly, the fountain taking its rise in the divine and far-famed city of David, in Sion the glorious; in it the law is fulfilled and the spiritual law is portrayed. In Sion, Christ the Law-giver consummated the typical pasch, and God, the Author of the old and the new dispensation, gave us the true pasch. In it the Lamb of God, who takes away the sins of the world, initiated His disciples unto His mystical feast, and gave them Himself slain as a victim, and the grape pressed in the true vine. In Sion, Christ is seen by His apostles, risen from the dead, and Thomas is told, and through Thomas the world, that He is Lord and God, having in Himself two natures after His resurrection, and consequently two operations, independent wills, enduring for all ages. Sion is the crown of churches, the resting-place of disciples. In it the echo of the Holy Spirit, the gift of tongues, His fiery descent are transmitted to the apostles. In it St John, taking the Mother of God, ministered to her wants. Sion is the mother of churches in the whole world, who offered a resting-place to the Mother of God after her Son's resurrection from the dead. In it, lastly, the Blessed Virgin was stretched on a small bed.

When I had reached this point of my discourse, I was obliged to give vent to my own feelings, and burning with loving desire, to shed reverent yet joyful tears, embracing, as it were, the bed so happy and blest and wondrous, which received the life-giving tabernacle and rejoiced in the contact of holiness. I seemed to take into my arms that holy and sacred body itself, worthy of God, and pressing my eyes, lips, and forehead, head, and cheeks to hers, I felt as if she was really there, though I was unable to see with my eyes what I desired. How, then, was she assumed to the heavenly courts? In this way. What were the honours then conferred upon her by God who commands us to honour our parents? The cloud which enclosed Jerusalem as with a net, by the divine commands, brought together eagles from the ends of the earth, those who are spread over the world, fishing for men in the various and numerous tongues of the spirit. By the net of the word they are saving men from the abyss of doubt and bringing them to the spiritual and heavenly table of the sacred and mystical banquet, the perfect marriage feast of the Divine Bridegroom, which the Father celebrates with His Son, who is equal to Himself and of the same nature. 'Where the spirit is,' says Christ the Truth, 'there shall the eagles be gathered together.' If we have already spoken concerning the second great and splendid coming of Him who spoke these words, it will not be out of place here by way of condiment.

Eye-witnesses, then, and ministers of the word were there, duly ministering to His Mother, and drawing from her a rich inheritance, as it were, and a full measure of praise. For is it a matter of doubt to any one that she is the source of blessing and the fountain of all good? Their followers and successors also were there, joining in their ministry and in their praise. A common labour produces common fruits. A chosen band from Jerusalem were there. It was fitting that the foremost men and prophets of the old law, they who had foretold God the Word's saving birth of her in time, should be there as a guard of honour. Nor did the angelic choirs fail. They who obeyed the king heartily (κατα γνωμην), and consequently were honoured by standing near Him, had the right to serve as a body-guard to His Mother, according to the flesh, the truly blessed and blissful one, surpassing all generations and all creation. All those were with her who are the brightness and the shining of the spirit, with spiritual eyes fixed upon her in reverence, and fear, and pure desire.

We hear divine and inspired words, and spiritual canticles appropriate to the parting hour. On this account it was meet to praise His boundless goodness, His immeasurable greatness, His omnipotence, the generosity surpassing all measure in His dealings with us, the overflowing riches of His mercy, the abyss of His tenderness; how, putting aside His greatness, He descended to our littleness with the co-operation of the Father and the Holy Spirit. Again, the supersubstantial One is supersubstantially created in the virginal womb. Being God He became man, and remains according to this union perfect God and perfect man, not giving up the substance of His Godhead nor ceasing to be of the same flesh and blood as we are. He, who fills all things and governs the universe with one word, took up His abode in a narrow place, and the material body of this blessed one received the burning fire of the Godhead, and as genuine gold it remained intact. This has taken place because God willed it, since His good pleasure makes things possible which could not happen without it. Then followed a strife of praise, not as if each was seeking to outdo the other—for this is vainglorious and far from pleasing to God—but as if they would leave nothing undone for the glory of God and the honour of God's Mother.

Then Adam and Eve, our first parents, opened their lips to exclaim, 'Thou blessed daughter of ours, who hast removed the penalty of our disobedience! Thou, inheriting from us a mortal body, hast won us immortality. Thou, taking thy being from us, hast given us back the being in grace. Thou hast conquered pain and loosened the bondage of death. Thou hast restored us to our former state. We had shut the door of paradise; thou didst find entrance to the tree of life. Through us sorrow came out of good; through thee good from sorrow. How canst thou who art all fair taste of death? Thou art the gate of life and the ladder to heaven. Death is become the passage to immortality. O thou truly blessed one! who that is not the Word could have borne what thou hast borne?'*

All the company of the saints exclaimed, 'Thou hast fulfilled our predictions. Thou hast purchased our present joy for us. Through thee we have broken the chains of death. Come to us, divine and life-giving receptacle. Come, our desire, thou who hast gained us our desire.'

And the saints standing by added their no less burning words: 'Remain with us, our comfort, our sole joy in this world. O Mother leave us not orphans who have suffered on thy Son's account. May we have thee as a refuge and refreshment in our labours and weariness. Thou canst remain if thou so willest, even as thou canst depart hence. If thou departest, O dwelling-place of God, let us go too, if we are thine through thy Son. Thou art our sole consolation on earth. We live as long as thou livest, and it is bliss to die with thee. Why do we speak of death? Death is life to thee, and better than life—

---

* ὄντως μακαρία σύ, παμμακάριστε. Τίς γὰρ, εἰ μήτιγε ὁ λόγος ἣ προσενήνεκται τοῦτο πάσχων, ὃ πράττειν ὑπείληπται.

incomparably exceeding this life. How is our life—life, if we are deprived of thee?'

The apostles and all the assembly of the Church may well have addressed some such words to the blessed Virgin. When they saw the Mother of God near her end and longing for it, they were moved by divine grace to sing farewell hymns, and wrapt out of the flesh, they sighed to accompany the dying Mother of God, and anticipated death through intensity of will. When they had all satisfied their duty of loving reverence and had woven her a rich crown of hymns, they spoke a parting blessing over her, as a God-given treasure, and the last words. These, I should think, were significant of this life's fleetingness, and of its leading to the hidden mysteries of future goods.

This, it appears to me, is what they did at once and unanimously. The King was there to receive with divine embrace * the holy, undefiled, and stainless soul of His Mother on her going home. And she, as we may well conjecture, said, 'Into Thy hands, O my Son, I commend my spirit. Receive my soul, dear

* χερσὶ θείαις καὶ ἀκηράτοις. Obscure when applied to our Lord.

to Thee, which Thou didst keep spotless. I
give my body to Thee, not to the earth.
Guard that which Thou wert pleased to inhabit and to preserve in virginity. Take me
to Thyself, that wherever Thou art, the fruit
of my womb, there I too may be. I am impelled to Thee who didst descend to me. Do
Thou be the consolation of my most cherished
children, whom Thou didst vouchsafe to call
Thy brethren, when my death leaves them in
loneliness. Bless them afresh through my
hands.' Then stretching out her hands, as
we may believe, she blessed all those present,
and then she heard the words: 'Come, my
beloved Mother, to thy rest. Arise and come,
most dear amongst women, the winter is past
and gone, the harvest time is at hand.* Thou
art fair, my beloved, and there is no stain in
thee. Thy fragrance is sweeter than all ointments.' With these words in her ear, that
holy one gave up her spirit into the hands of
her Son.

What happens? Nature, I conjecture, is
stirred to its depths, strange sounds and voices
are heard, and the swelling hymns of angels

---

* ὁ καιρὸς τῆς τομῆς ἔφθασε.

who precede, accompany, and follow her. Some constitute the guard of honour to that undefiled and immaculate ($\pi a\nu a\gamma i\alpha$) soul on its way to heaven until the queen reaches the divine throne. Others surrounding the sacred and divine body proclaim God's Mother in angelic harmony. What of those who watched by the most holy and immaculate ($\pi a\nu a\gamma i\omega$) body? In loving reverence and with tears of joy they gathered round the blessed and divine tabernacle, embracing every member, and were filled with holiness and thanksgiving. Then illnesses were cured, and demons were put to flight and banished to the regions of darkness. The air and atmosphere and heavens were sanctified by her passage through them, the earth by the burial of her body. Nor was water deprived of a blessing. She was washed in pure water. It did not cleanse her, but was rather itself sanctified. Then, hearing was given to the deaf, the lame recovered their feet, and the blind their sight. Sinners who approached with faith blotted out the handwriting against them. Then the holy body is wrapped in a snow-white winding-sheet, and the queen is again laid upon her bed. Then follow lights and incense and hymns, and angels singing as befits the solemnity; apostles and patriarchs acclaiming her in inspired song.

When the Ark of God, departing from Mount Sion for the heavenly country, was borne on the shoulders of the Apostles, it was placed on the way in the tomb. First it was taken through the city, as a bride dazzling with spiritual radiance, and then carried to the sacred place of Gethsemane, angels overshadowing it with their wings, going before, accompanying, and following it, together with the whole assembly of the Church. King Solomon compelled all the elders of Israel in Sion to bear the ark of the covenant of the Lord from the city of David, that is Sion, to rest in the temple of the Lord, which he had built, and the priests took the ark and the tabernacle of the testimony, and the priests and levites raised it. And the king and all the people sacrificed numberless oxen and sheep before the ark. And the priests carried in the ark of the testimony of God into its place, into the Holy of Holies, beneath the wings of the cherubim. So is it now with the dwelling-place of the true ark, no longer of the testimony, but the very substance of God the Word. The new Solomon, the Prince of peace, the Creator of all things in the heavens and on the earth, assembled together to-day the supporters of the new covenant, that is the Apostles, with all the people of the saints in Jerusalem, brought in her soul through angels to the true Holy of Holies, under the wings of the four living creatures, and set her on His throne within the veil, where Christ Himself had preceded her. Her body the while is borne by the Apostles' hands, the King of Kings covering her with the splendour of His invisible Godhead, the whole assembly of the saints preceding her, with sacred song and sacrifice of praise until through the tomb it was placed in the delights of Eden, the heavenly tabernacles.

Perchance, Jews also were there, if any, not too reprobate were to be found. It will not be beside the mark to mention here a thing that is asserted by many. It is said that when those, who were carrying the blessed body of God's Mother, had reached the descent of the opposite mountains, a certain Jew, the slave of sin, and pledged by his folly, imitated the servant of Caiphas, who struck the divine Face of Christ our Lord and Master, and made himself the devil's instrument. Full of wicked passion and malice, he rushed at that most divine tabernacle, which angels approached with fear, and impiously dragged the bier with both his hands to the ground. This was prompted by the envy of the arch enemy, but his labours were in vain, and he reaped a severe and fitting reminder of his deed. It is said that he lost the use of his hands, which had perpetrated his malicious deed, until faith moved him to repentance. The bearers were standing near. The wretched man placed his hands on the wondrous and life-giving tabernacle, and they again became sound. Circumstances had made him wise, as often happens. But let us return to our subject.

Then they reached the most sacred Gethsemane, and once more there were embracings and prayers and panegyrics, hymns and tears, poured forth by sorrowful and loving hearts. They mingled a flood of weeping and sweating.* And thus the immaculate (πανάγιον)

---

* καὶ ἦν ἰδεῖν ἰδρῶτας καὶ δάκρυα τοῖς χεύμασιν ἀμιλλώμενα.

body was laid in the tomb. Then it was assumed after three days to the heavenly mansions. The bosom of the earth was no fitting receptacle for the Lord's dwelling-place, the living source of cleansing water, the corn of heavenly bread, the sacred vine of divine wine, the evergreen and fruitful olive-branch of God's mercy. And just as the all holy body of God's Son, which was taken from her, rose from the dead on the third day, it followed that she should be snatched from the tomb, that the mother should be united to her Son; and as He had come down to her, so she should be raised up to Him, into the more perfect dwelling-place, heaven itself. It was meet that she, who had sheltered God the Word in her own womb, should inhabit the tabernacles of her Son. And as our Lord said it behoved Him to be concerned with His Father's business, so it behoved His mother that she should dwell in the courts of her Son, in the house of the Lord, and in the courts of the house of our God. If all those who rejoice dwell in Him, where must the cause itself of joy abide? It was fitting that the body of her, who preserved her virginity unsullied in her motherhood, should be kept from corruption even after death. She who nursed her Creator as an infant at her breast, had a right to be in the divine tabernacles. The place of the bride whom the Father had espoused, was in the heavenly courts. It was fitting that she who saw her Son die on the cross, and received in her heart the sword of pain which she had not felt in childbirth, should gaze upon Him seated next to the Father. The Mother of God had a right to the possession of her Son, and as handmaid and Mother of God to the worship of all creation. The inheritance of the parents ever passes to the children. Now, as a wise man said, the sources of sacred waters are above. The Son made all creation serve His Mother.

Let us then also keep solemn feast to-day to honour the joyful departure of God's Mother, not with flutes nor corybants, nor the orgies of Cybele, the mother of false gods, as they say, whom foolish people talk of as a fruitful mother of children, and truth as no mother at all. These are demons and false imaginings. They usurp what they are not by nature to impose upon human folly. For how can what is bodiless lead the wedded life*? How can that be god which, not being before, is present only after birth? That devils were bodiless is apparent to all, even to those who are intellectually blind. Homer somewhere testifies to the condition of the gods he honours:

> They eat not barley, and drink not ruddy wine,
> So they are bloodless and are called immortal.

They eat not bread, he says, neither do they drink fiery wine. On this account they are anæmic, that is, without blood, and are called immortals. He truly and appropriately says, 'are called.' They are called immortals They are not that which they are called. They died the death of wickedness. Now we worship God, not God beginning His being, but who always was and is above all cause and argument or created mind or nature. We honour and reverence the Mother of God, not ascribing to her the eternal generation of His Godhead. For the generation of God the Word was not in time, and was co-eternal with the Father. We acknowledge a second generation in His spontaneous taking flesh, and we see and know the cause of this. He

* γεννᾷ γὰρ πῶς ἐκ συνδυασμοῦ τὸ ἀσώματον; καὶ τίνα τρόπον μιχθήσεται.

who is without beginning and without body takes flesh for us as one of ourselves. And taking flesh of this sacred Virgin, He is born without man, remaining Himself perfect God, and becoming perfect man, perfect God in His flesh, and perfect Man in His Godhead. Thus, recognising God's Mother in this Virgin, we celebrate her falling asleep, not proclaiming her as God—far be from us these heathen fables—since we are announcing her death, but recognising her as the Mother of the Incarnate God.

O people of Christ, let us acclaim her to-day in sacred song, acknowledge our own good fortune and proclaim it. Let us honour her in nocturnal vigil; let us delight in her purity of soul and body, for she next to God surpasses all in purity. It is natural for similar things to glory in each other. Let us show our love for her by compassion and kindness towards the poor. For if mercy is the best worship of God, who will refuse to show His Mother devotion in the same way? She opened to us the unspeakable abyss of God's love for us. Through her the old enmity against the Creator is destroyed. Through her our reconciliation with Him is strengthened, peace and grace are given to us, men are the companions of angels, and we, who were in dishonour, are made the children of God. From her we have plucked the fruit of life. From her we have received the seed of immortality. She is the channel of all our goods. In her God was man and man was God. What more marvellous or more blessed? I approach the subject in fear and trembling. With Mary, the prophetess, O youthful souls, let us sound our musical instruments, mortifying our members on earth, for this is spiritual music. Let our souls rejoice in the Ark of God, and the walls of Jericho will yield, I mean the fortresses of the enemy. Let us dance in spirit with David; to-day the Ark of God is at rest. With Gabriel, the great archangel, let us exclaim, 'Hail, full of grace, the Lord is with thee. Hail, inexhaustible ocean of grace. Hail, sole refuge in grief. Hail, cure of hearts. Hail, through whom death is expelled and life is installed.'

And you I will speak to as if living, most sacred of tombs, after the life-giving tomb of our Lord, which is the source of the resurrection.

Where is the pure gold which apostolic hands confided to you? Where is the inexhaustible treasure? Where the precious receptacle of God? Where is the living table? Where the new book in which the incomprehensible Word of God is written without hands? Where is the abyss of grace and the ocean of healing? Where is the life-giving fountain? Where is the sweet and loved body of God's Mother?

Why* do you seek in the tomb one who has been assumed to the heavenly courts? Why do you make me responsible for not keeping her? I was powerless to go against the divine commands. That sacred and holy body, leaving the winding-sheet behind, filled me full of sweet fragrance, sanctified me by its contact, and fulfilled the divine scheme, and was then assumed, angels and archangels and all the heavenly powers escorting it. Now angels surround me, and divine grace abounds in me. I am the physician of the sick. I am a perpetual source of health, and the terror of demons. I am a city of refuge for fugitives. Approach with faith and you will receive a sea of graces. Come, you of weak faith. All you

* The supposed answer of the tomb.

that thirst, come to the waters in obedience to Isaias' commands, and you who have no money, come and buy for nothing. I call upon all with the Gospel invitation. Let him who longs for bodily or spiritual cure, forgiveness of sins, deliverance from misfortune, the possession of heaven, approach me with faith, and draw hence a strong and rich stream of grace. Just as the action of one and the same water acts differently on the earth, air, and sun, according to the nature of each, producing wine in the vine and oil in the olive-tree, so does one and the same grace profit each person according to his needs. I do not possess grace on my own account. A tomb given up to corruption, an object of sorrow and dejection, I receive a precious ointment, and am impregnated with it, and this sweet fragrance alters my condition whilst it lasts. Truly, divine graces flow where they will. I have sheltered the source of joy, and I have become rich in its perennial fountain.*

What shall we answer the tomb? You have indeed rich and abiding grace, but divine power is not restricted by place, neither is the Mother

* An unauthentic paragraph omitted.

of God's working. If it were confined to the tomb alone, few would be the richer. Now it is freely distributed in all parts of the world. Let us then make our memory serve as a storehouse of God's Mother. How shall this be? She is a virgin and a lover of virginity. She is pure and a lover of purity. If we purify our mind with the body, we shall possess her grace. She shuns all impurity and impure passions. She has a horror of intemperance, and a special hatred for fornication. She turns from its allurements as from the progeny of serpents . . . She looks upon all sin as death-inflicting, rejoicing in all good. Contraries are cured by contraries. She delights in fasting and continence and spiritual canticles, in purity, virginity, and wisdom. With these she is ever at peace, and takes them to her heart. She embraces peace and a meek spirit, and love, mercy, and humility as her children. In a word, she grieves over every sin, and is glad at all goodness as if it were her own. If we turn away from our former sins in all earnestness and love goodness with all our hearts, and make it our constant companion, she will frequently visit her servants, bringing all blessings with her, Christ her Son, the King and Lord who reigns in our hearts. To Him be glory, praise, honour, power, and magnificence, with the eternal Father and the Holy Spirit, now and for ever.

SERMON III.

ON THE ASSUMPTION (κοίμησις).

LOVERS are wont to speak of what they love, and to let their fancy run on it by day and night. Let no one therefore blame me, if I add a third tribute to the Mother of God, on her triumphant departure. I am not profiting her, but myself and you who are here present, putting before you a spiritual seasoning and refreshment in keeping with this holy night. We are suffering, as you see, from scarcity of eatables. Therefore I am extemporising a repast, which, if not very costly nor worthy of the occasion, will certainly be sufficient to still hunger. She does not need our praise. It is we who need her glory. How indeed can glory be glorified, or the source of light be enlightened? We are weaving a crown for ourselves in the doing. 'I live,' the Lord says, 'and I will glorify those who glorify Me.'

Wine is truly pleasant to drink, and bread to eat. The one rejoices, the other strengthens the heart of man. But what is sweeter than the Mother of my God? She has taken my mind captive, and held my tongue in bondage. I think of her by day and night. She, the Mother of the Word, supplies my words. The fruit of sterility makes sterile minds fruitful. We keep to-day the feast of her blessed and divine transit from this world. Let us then climb up the mystical mountain, where beyond the reach of worldly things, passing through the obscurity of storm, we stand in the divine light and may give praise to Almighty power. How does He, who dwells in the splendour of His glory, descend into the Virgin's womb without leaving the bosom of the Father? How is He conceived in the flesh, and does He spontaneously suffer, and suffer unto death, in that material body, gaining immortality through corruptibility? (φθορᾷ κτησάμενος τὸ ἄφθαρτον). And, again, ascending to the Father, He drew His Mother, according to the flesh, to His own Father, assuming into the heavenly country her who was heaven on earth.

To-day the living ladder, through whom the

Most High descended and was seen on earth, and conversed with men, was assumed into heaven by death. To-day the heavenly table, she, who contained the bread of life, the fire of the Godhead, without knowing man, was assumed from earth to heaven, and the gates of heaven opened wide to receive the gate of God from the East. To-day the living city of God is transferred from the earthly to the heavenly Jerusalem, and she, who, conceived her first-born and only Son, the first-born of all creation, the only begotten of the Father, rests in the Church of the first-born: the true and living Ark of the Lord is taken to the peace of her Son. The gates of heaven are opened to receive the receptacle of God, who, bringing forth the tree of life, destroyed Eve's disobedience and Adam's penalty of death. And Christ, the cause of all life, receives the chosen mirror, the mountain from which the stone without hands filled the whole earth. She, who brought about the Word's divine Incarnation, rests in her glorious tomb as in a bridal-chamber, whence she goes to the heavenly bridals, to share in the kingdom of her Son and God, leaving her tomb as a place of rest for those on earth. Is her tomb indeed a resting-place? Yes, more famous than any other, not shining with gold, or silver, or precious stones, nor covered with silken, golden, or purple adornments, but with the divine radiance of the Holy Spirit. The angelic state is not for lovers of this world, but the wondrous life of the blessed is for the servants of the Spirit, and passing to God is better and sweeter than any other life. This tomb is fairer than Eden. And that I may not speak of the enemy's deceit, in the one; of his, so to say, clever counsel, his envy and covetousness, of Eve's weakness and pliability, the bait, sure and tempting, which cheated her and her husband, their disobedience, exile, and death, not to speak of these things so as not to turn our feast into sorrow, *this* grave gave up the mortal body it contained to the heavenly country. Eve became the mother of the human family, and is not man made after the divine image, convicted by her condemnation; 'earth thou art, and unto earth thou shalt return.' This tomb is more precious than the tabernacle of old, receiving the real and life-giving receptacle of the Lord, the heavenly table, not the loaves of proposition, but of heaven, not material fire, but her who contained the pure fire of the Godhead. This tomb is holier than the ark of Moses, blessed not with types and shadows, but the truth itself. It showed forth the pure and golden urn, containing the heavenly manna, the living tablet, receiving the Incarnate Word of God from the impress of the Holy Spirit, the golden censer of the supersubstantial word. It showed forth her who conceived the divine fire embalming all creation.

Let demons take to flight, and the thrice miserable Nestorians perish as the Egyptians of old, and their ruler Pharao, the younger, a cruel devastator. They were swallowed up in the abyss of blasphemy. Let us who are saved with dry feet, crossing the bitter waters of impiety, raise our voices to the Mother of God at her departure. Let Mary, personifying the Church, lead the joyful strain. Let the maidens of the spiritual Jerusalem go out in singing choirs. Let kings and judges, with rulers, youths, and virgins, young and old, proclaim the Mother of God, and all peoples and nations in their different ways and tongues, sing a new canticle. Let the air resound with praise and instrument, and the sun gladden this day of salvation. Rejoice, O heavens, and may the clouds rain justice. Be glad, O divine apostles, the chosen ones of God's flock, who seem to reach the highest visions, as lofty mountain tops. And you God's sheep, and His holy people, the flock of the Church, who look to the high mountains of perfection, be sad, for the fountain of life, God's Mother, is dead. It was necessary that what was made of earth should return to earth, and thus be assumed to heaven. It was fitting that the earthly tenement should be cast off, as gold is purified, so that the flesh in death might become pure and immortal, and rise in shining immortality from the tomb.

To-day she begins her second life through Him who was the cause of her first being. She gave a beginning, I mean, the life of the body, to Him who had no beginning in time, although the Father was the cause of His divine existence. Rejoice holy and divine Mount Sion, in which reposes the living divine mountain, the new Bethel, with its grace, human nature united with the Godhead. From thee her Son ascended to heaven as from the olives. Let the world-embracing cloud be prepared and the winds gather the apostles to Mount Sion from the ends of the earth. Who are these who soar up as clouds and eagles to the cause of all resurrection, ministering to the Mother of God? Who is she who rises resplendent, all pure, and bright as the sun? Let the spiritual lyres sing to her, the apostolic tongues. Let grave theologians raise their voices in praise, Hierotheus, the vessel of election, in whom the Holy Spirit abides, knowing and teaching divine things by the divine indwelling. Let him be wrapt out of the body and join willingly in the joyful hymn. Let all nations clap their hands and praise the Mother of God. Let angels minister to her body. Follow your Queen, O daughters of Jerusalem, and, together with her virgins in the spirit, approach your Bridegroom in order to sit at His right hand. Make haste, Lord, to give Thy Mother the welcome which is her due. Stretch out Thy divine hands. Receive Thy Mother's soul into the Father's hands unto which Thou didst commend Thy spirit on the Cross. Speak sweet words to her:

'Come, my beloved, whose purity is more dazzling than the sun, thou gavest me of thy own, receive now what is mine. Come, my Mother, to thy Son, reign with Him who was poor with thee.' Depart, O Queen, depart, not as Moses did who went up to die. Die rather that thou mayest ascend. Give up thy soul into the hands of thy Son. Return earth to the earth, it will be no obstacle. Lift up your eyes, O people of God. See in Sion the Ark of the Lord God of powers, and the apostles standing by it, burying the life-giving body which received our Lord. Invisible angels are all around in lowly reverence doing homage to the Mother of their Lord. The Lord Himself is there, who is present everywhere, and filling all things, the universal Being, not in place. He is the Author and Creator of all things. Behold the Virgin, the daughter of Adam and Mother of God; through Adam she gives her body to the earth, her soul to her Son above in the heavenly courts. Let the holy city be sanctified, and rejoice in eternal praise. Let angels precede the divine tabernacle on its passage, and prepare the tomb. Let the radiance of the spirit adorn it. Let sweet ointment be made ready and poured over the pure and undefiled body. Let a clear stream of grace flow from grace in its source. Let the earth be sanctified by contact with that body. Let the air rejoice at the Assumption. Let gentle breezes waft grace. Let all nature keep the feast of the Mother of God's Assumption. May youthful bands applaud and eloquent tongues acclaim her, and wise hearts ponder on the wonder, priests hoary with age gather strength at the sight. Let all creation emulate heaven, even so the true measure of rejoicing would not be reached.

Come, let us depart with her. Come, let us descend to that tomb with all our heart's desire. Let us draw round that most sacred bed and sing the sweet words, 'Hail, full of grace, the Lord is with thee. Hail, predestined Mother of God. Hail, thou chosen one in the design of God from all eternity, most sacred hope of earth, resting-place of divine fire, holiest delight of the Spirit, fountain of living water, paradise of the tree of life, divine vine-branch, bringing forth soul-sustaining nectar and ambrosia. Full river of spiritual graces, fertile land of the divine pastures, rose of purity, with the sweet fragrance of grace, lily of the royal robe, pure Mother of the Lamb of God who takes away the sins of the world, token of our redemption, handmaid and Mother, surpassing angelic powers.' Come, let us stand round that pure tomb and draw grace to our hearts. Let us raise the ever-virginal body with spiritual arms, and go with her into the grave to die with her. Let us renounce our passions, and live with her in purity, listening to the divine canticles of angels in the heavenly courts. Let us go in adoring, and learn the wondrous mystery by which she is assumed to heaven, to be with her Son, higher than all the angelic choirs. No one stands between Son and Mother. This, O Mother of God, is my third sermon on thy departure, in lowly reverence to the Holy Trinity to whom thou didst minister, the goodness of the Father, the power of the Spirit, receiving the Uncreated Word, the Almighty Wisdom and Power of God. Accept, then, my good-will, which is greater than my capacity, and give us salvation. Heal our passions, cure our diseases, help us out of our difficulties, make our lives peaceful, send us the illumination of the Spirit. Inflame us with the desire of thy Son. Render us pleasing to Him, so that we may enjoy happiness with Him, seeing thee resplendent with thy Son's glory, rejoicing for ever, keeping feast in the Church with those who worthily celebrate Him who worked our salvation through thee, Christ the Son of God, and our God. To Him be glory and majesty, with the uncreated Father and the all-holy and life-giving Spirit, now and for ever, through the endless ages of eternity. Amen.

INDEX

Abraham and sons of Emmor, 9; image of God, 123.
Adam and Eve addressing Our Lady, 183.
Ambrose of Milan, St, on Incarnation, 136.
Amphilochius, addressed by St Basil, 34.
Angarus, King of Edessa, 33.
Angelic nature not taken by God, 102.
Anne, St, her name, 156.
Ark of God, the true, 168, 188; at rest, 195.
Assumption of Our Lady, 202, 207, 209, 210.
Athanasius, Archbishop of Antioch, 141.
Athanasius, St, his testimony, 120.
Augustine, St, *de Civitate Dei*, 57.

Babylon, three children in, 132.
Baltasar, impiety of, 110.
Basil, St, on Tradition, 28; on St Gordion, 37; on Forty Martyrs, 117.
Berenice of Paneada, 124.
Body of Christ in Holy Eucharist, 102.
Brazen Serpent, image of the Cross, 50.
Burial of Our Lady, 190, 191, 208.
Burning bush, image of Our Lady, 79.

Cherubim, image of, 14.
Chrysostom, St John, his testimony, 83, 118, 121; on the Machabees, 137; to Julian the Apostate, 138.
Church assailed by enemies, 1.

Constantine, zeal for images, 126.
Cross, veneration of, 78, 130, 134.
Cyril of Alexandria, St, 121.
Cyril of Jerusalem, 137; to Julian the Apostate, 138.

Daniel and David, worship of, 13.
Denis the Areopagite, 10; on images, 31, 96.
Denis, St, of Athens, 116.
Deuteronomy, testimony of, 6, 63.
Divine things clothed in form, 99.

Egyptians, their burial, 29.
Elias taken to heaven, 166.
Eliseus, a wonder-worker, 45.
Epiphanius, St, on images, 29, 77.
Eupraxia, St, 51.
Ezechiel, his vision, 46, 128, 162.

Forty martyrs, 38, 40, 117.
Francis de Sales, St, on the Cross, 47.

Gabriel, St, sent to Mary, 157.
Godhead, not to be represented, 5, 8, 9, 14, 15, 62, 67, 98.
Gregory of Nazianzen, St, 122.
Gregory of Nyssa, St, 41.

Holy places, 109; things, 110.
Homer, on the gods, 193.

Idolatry of Israelites, 80.
Idol worship of heathens, 77.
Images, dishonour shown to, 68, 86; worship of, 74, 75, 89; definition of, 92; kinds, 93, 94, 95, 97, 106, 133; of saints, a fruitful worship, 112.
Invisible things through visible, 11.
Isaias, his vision of God, 100; virgin foretold by, 162.

Jacob, his worship, 9, 13, 131; typical, 27; receiving Joseph's cloak, 132; ladder of, 161.

INDEX.

Jews, their proneness to idolatry, 8.
Jezabel, punishment of, 70.
Joachim, St, 154.
Jordan, stones of, 20, 97.
Joseph, worshipped by brothers, 14.
Josue, worshipped an angel, 101.

King's image, value of, 136 ; kings not legislators in the Church, 52, 69, 76.

Latreia, worship of, 7 ; given to God alone, 64, 104, 107.
Law, image of the future, 82, 140 ; observances of, 18 ; images of, 46, 49, 81, 88 ; superseded by grace, 73.
Leo of Neapolis, on the Cross, 43.

Matter not despicable, 17, 71, 72 ; consecrated, 127.
Mary of Egypt, St, praying to Our Lady, 51, 143, 145.
Maximus, St, his testimony, 84.
Methodius, St, on images, 145.
Moses, testimony of, 53, 60, 65 ; worships Jethor, 134.
Mother of God, 12 ; images of, 97 ; worship of, 54, 91 ; death of, 164, 186 ; her Assumption, 166, 167, 173, 176 ; the city of God, 148 ; her praises, 150 ; her birth, 150 ; her presentation, 156 ; her grace, 158 ; her virginity, 159, 173 ; a spiritual Eden, 160 ; her intercession, what, 169 ; the new Eden, 174 ; heaven, 175 ; her death, painless, 177 ; eye-witnesses of, 181 ; saint of saints, 178 ; her right to worship of all, 192 ; heavenly bridals of, 203 ; fountain of life, 206.

Our Lord's human birth, 194.

Persecutors of saints punished, 70.
Peter, St, chief of apostles, 26.
Pharao worshipped by Jacob, 9.

Saints, why honoured, 21, 23, 24 ; their shadow, 113 ; our worship of, 108.

Scripture, true interpretation of, 66.
Severianus, on the Cross, 139.
Simon Stylites, St, venerated in Rome, 119.
Sion, what, 179
Solomon and the temple, 22, 45, 129.
Spiritual conceptions through corporeal things, 90.

Tomb of Our Lady, 196, 197, 205, 210; fairer than Eden, 204.

Tradition, ancient, 114; unwritten, 75.
Types, honourable, 142.

Worship, false, 56, 57, 58; kinds of, 104, 105, 106, 108, 111.

www.ingramcontent.com/pod-product-compliance
Lightning Source LLC
Chambersburg PA
CBHW021836230426
43669CB00008B/985